WHAT MARY & JOSEPH KNEW ABOUT PARENTING

SURPRISING INSIGHTS FROM

THE BEST *(and Worst)* PARENTS IN THE BIBLE

Rick Osborne

INTEGRITY®
PUBLISHERS

family

Nashville

What Mary & Joseph Knew About Parenting:
Surprising Insights from the Best (and Worst) Parents in the Bible

Published by Integrity Publishers, a division of Integrity Media, Inc., 5250 Virginia Way, Suite 110, Brentwood, TN 37027.

HELPING PEOPLE WORLDWIDE EXPERIENCE *the* MANIFEST PRESENCE *of* GOD.

Cover Design:
Brand Navigation, The Office of Bill Chiaravalle, www.officeofbc.com
Interior Design:
Teresa Billingsley/Nashville, TN

Library of Congress Cataloging-in-Publication Data
Osborne, Rick.
What Mary and Joseph knew about parenting / by Rick Osborne.
p. cm.
Summary: "Examples and principles from the Bible that can help today's parents in raising children the way God intended"—Provided by the publisher.

ISBN 1-59145-288-0 (tradepaper)

1. Parenting—Biblical teaching. 2. Child rearing—Biblical teaching. 3. Parenting—Religious aspects—Christianity. 4. Child rearing—Religious aspects—Christianity. 5. Mary, Blessed Virgin, Saint. 6. Joseph, Saint.

I. Title.
BV4529.O684   2005
248.8'45—dc22   2005003141

Printed in the United States of America
05 06 07 08 09 DPS 9 8 7 6 5 4 3 2 1

DEDICATION

To Dr. James Dobson who has, through his efforts and undying commitment, blazed a trail for and inspired an army of us who now work to strengthen families in Christ.

SPECIAL THANKS

Although only one name usually goes on the cover of a book, in truth most are the results of a talented team. I am very thankful for the team that worked with me on this book: Laura Minchew, who is one of the best at what she does, not only believed in the project and encouraged me forward but provided valuable insight and ideas and flawless team leadership—thank you Laura, for shaping the vision and making this book possible; Steve Halliday worked tirelessly to edit and trim and clarify my text, wonderfully crafting my enormous piles of words and thoughts into a seamless, accurate and to-the-point read—thank you Steve, you are obviously enormously gifted in many ways and I greatly appreciate your help; last but not least, Mikal Marrs, my assistant who is a gift from God to me. Thank you Mikal, for all that you do—I'm quite sure that most of what I do would not get done without your indispensable support.

PARENTING BY THE BOOK

"For everything that was written in the past was written to teach us, so that through endurance and the encouragement of the scriptures we might have hope" (Romans 15:4).

Contents

Part Two

The New Testament: The Results of Parenting by the Book

Introduction

Parenting by the Book

*H*ave you ever wondered why God chose Mary and Joseph to parent his only beloved Son? Was it just because they came from the right family line? If Jesus' upbringing did not depend on human parenting, did it even matter *whom* in that family line the Lord chose? Or, if it *did* matter, did God choose them because he knew they would be great parents?

At this point you might be saying, "This is *Jesus* we're talking about. He would have been the perfect child, even with the worst parents to ever strap on the title." Surely Jesus must have supernaturally parented himself—just add food, shelter, and clothing.

That would be true *if* God had set things up that way. God's Word teaches us, however, that he had a different plan.

Even though he was God in the flesh, Jesus had to grow and learn just like any other child. For all intents and purposes, he was a regular child with regular parents, raised the regular way. As our High Priest, in fact, Jesus needed to identify with us in every way—and how could that not include how he was raised?

> *For this reason **he had to be made like his brothers in every way**, in order that he might become a merciful and faithful high priest in service to God, and that he might make atonement for the sins of the people. Because he himself suffered when he was tempted, he is able to help those who are being tempted."*
> (Hebrews 2:17–18, emphasis added)

Since God wanted Jesus to be raised in the regular way, he needed great parents. Or more specifically, he needed parents who would raise Jesus as God's Word instructs moms and dads to raise their children. Would it surprise you to learn that God set this up ahead of time and told Abraham about it?

> *Abraham will surely become a great and powerful nation, and all nations on earth will be blessed through him. **For I have chosen him, so that he will direct his children and his household after him to keep the way of the LORD** by doing what is right and just so that the LORD will bring about for Abraham what he has promised him.* (Genesis 18:18–19, emphasis added)

God chose Abraham and Sarah because he wanted a couple that would raise their children to serve him—to parent God's way, in other words. He wanted them to get it right not only with Isaac, but also to set in motion an example of raising children to be passed on through Isaac to his grandchildren and then to the whole nation of Israel—Abraham's descendants: ". . . *direct his children and his household **after him** . . .*" (Genesis 18:19). Here's where it gets interesting: God said that they needed to parent his way *"that the LORD will bring about for Abraham what he has promised him"* (Genesis 18:19c). In other words, God promised to shower the couple with his covenant blessings when they parented God's way.

What exactly did God promise Abraham? Look at verse 18: *"Abraham will surely become a great and powerful nation, and all nations on earth will be blessed through him."*

This promise ultimately referred, of course, to Jesus and to what God would accomplish through his birth, death, and resurrection. Through Jesus, a descendant of Abraham, all of the nations and people of the earth have an opportunity to receive God's forgiveness and blessing.

So why did God tell Abraham that he had to parent God's way if his descendants were to enjoy the blessings of this incredible promise? The answer takes us back to Mary and Joseph. The parenting lessons God taught Abraham and Sarah as parents got passed down from generation to generation. All through the Old Testament, God admonished his people to raise their children his way, and the Bible is full of examples both of those who did and of those who didn't bother. It brims with instructions on how to raise children God's way.

By the time Mary and Joseph got their turn to raise children, the Word of God contained all of the most important instruction they needed in order to raise Jesus God's way. Paul said it nicely: *"For everything that was written in the past was written to teach us"* (Romans 15:4).

Abraham got the "parenting God's way" ball rolling, and by so doing set the stage for Jesus to be "parented by the Book," thus fulfilling the promise God made to Abraham.

It's not hard to see that Mary and Joseph gleaned God's parenting secrets from his Word and followed them. In the Gospels we see them applying these truths. No passage lists Mary and Joseph's "seven keys to successful parenting," of course, but the written record clearly shows they knew the most important key: applying the parenting instructions, principles, and stories found in God's Word.

Think of the time the angel Gabriel told Mary that she would give birth to a miracle baby. She replied, *"I am the Lord's servant. May it be to me as you have said"* (Luke 1:38). The Greek word translated "servant" is essentially the same word in Hebrew that Samuel's mother, Hannah, used when she asked God for a son (1 Samuel 1:11).

Shortly after the angelic visitation, Mary visited her relative Elizabeth, already six months pregnant (with a baby who would come to be known as John the Baptist). As soon as Mary walked in the door, the Holy Spirit filled Elizabeth and revealed to her that the child Mary carried was the Messiah. Mary responded with a song of praise to God. The words of her song (Luke 1:46–56) borrow heavily from the prayer Hannah offered when she dedicated her young son, Samuel, to God's service in the tabernacle (1 Samuel 2:1–10).

Mary's much-applauded response—and her humble, obedient attitude toward her unexpected role as the mother of the Messiah—came out of a heart obviously familiar with Hannah's story in God's Word.

God invented parenting, and he has wonderfully filled the Bible, from Genesis to Revelation, with parenting examples and principles that can help us raise children the way he meant them to be raised.

As I scoured the Bible and studied what "Mary and Joseph Knew About Parenting," I felt amazed at the wealth of teaching that God's Word contains on the topic. And as I began to apply what I learned, I saw tremendous results in the lives of my children.

God didn't cause these examples to be written down for the sake of Mary and Joseph alone; they found a place in Scripture to instruct today's Christian parents, as well. Mary and Joseph provide a great example for us of striving to learn and apply God's parenting secrets.

Remember, we're still seeing God's promise to Abraham come to pass. One key to seeing all nations blessed is passing the torch to the next generation. We all die sooner or later, and the next generation must continue to carry the torch in order to bring the Good News to all the nations.

Mary and Joseph did not "coincidentally" land in the right place at the right time. God chose them and prepared them for a mind-boggling task. That task to raise God's children has been passed on to us.

We, too, need to learn from Hannah.

Because God has called us to raise his chosen children, we need attitudes appropriate to his honored servants. Christian parenting is an honored calling. Like Mary, we need to acknowledge that and, with God's help, put our all into learning to parent God's way.

I wrote this book with a passionate desire in my heart to see Christian parents everywhere learn how to raise their children God's way. I also wrote with practical application in mind. I pray that God would help us journey through the Bible and help us to clearly see the very hands-on, real-life parenting help that bursts from its pages.

One more thing before you turn the page: although you can profitably read this book from cover to cover in order to see the progression of God's parenting plan, you can also use the book as a handy reference or lifeline. Each essay stands on its own and deals with a separate topic—so feel free to dive in at a point of felt need, or wherever your curiosity may lead.

I pray that God will open his Word to your heart and that his parenting instructions will bless your family as much as they have mine—a blessing I have found incalculable.

Rick Osborne

PART ONE

THE OLD TESTAMENT: THE PARENTING BOOK OF MARY AND JOSEPH

CHAPTER 1

The
Third Parent:
Parenting with Help from Above

*W*ith just a few words, the book of Genesis paints an awesome picture of life with God in the Garden of Eden:

> *Then the man and his wife heard the sound of the LORD God as he was walking in the garden in the cool of the day.* (Genesis 3:8, NIV)

Before they sinned, Adam and Eve, the first parents, walked in paradise with God himself. Unfortunately, the first two human children, Cain and Abel, were born outside of Eden after Adam and Eve. They never had a chance to experience the kind of full, spiritual, emotional, and physical union with God that their parents enjoyed before their sin. And Adam and Eve never experienced the joys of parenting in God's full presence.

God's original design did not call for children to grow up estranged from him and only later to find their way back. He wanted each child to grow up with his boundless love and in his unveiled presence. But sin estranged every child ever born from the full experience of God's intimate "third parent" love—every child except one, of course. Jesus entered this world without sin. And here's the really good news: because of his sacrifice, every child can now receive God's forgiveness and enter into an intimate relationship with their loving heavenly Father.

We in the body of Christ have an awesome privilege: we can lead our children to Christ and raise them in an environment rich with God's presence, love, care, and teaching. We can't be with our children 24/7, but God can. We don't always know and/or understand how they're feeling or what they're going through, but God does.

I have a hard time counting how often I've felt concerned (or should I say, overly concerned) about one of my children, only to find comfort as I prayed, remembering that the Third Parent is with them. Yes, God wants us to pray about and for our children, and we can come to him boldly and with confidence, knowing that he loves our children even more than we ever could and that he's actively involved in parenting them. He always has his loving eye and hand on them.

Not only do we have the active blessing of God on our children as they grow up in his presence, but we also have God as our parenting partner. He's always right there with us, ready to guide us and teach us how to parent. The more we rely on him, the more success we will enjoy.

As I ponder the last eighteen years of parenting, I can do nothing but thank God for his awesome help. I think of the time he showed me that my little daughter had abandoned the truth in some matter, making it possible for me to lovingly teach and correct her before it became a habit. Or I recall the time my son asked in frustration, "Why can't I see God? Why does he hide from us?" As I stood there praying, the "just right" answer came to me, strengthening both my faith and his. Or I ponder the times I had to teach and/or discipline my kids, and God helped me to do it in such a way that they listened and learned. I even think of the many times God showed me when *I* got it wrong and then helped me to make it right.

God loves you and he doesn't expect you to be a perfect parent. But he *does* want you to include him and rely on him as the Third Parent. To be accurate, he's actually the FIRST Parent; he knew your children and what life would hold for them before they took their first breath (Psalm 139:16). When we refuse to react harshly, or deal out punishments, or make important decisions on our own, and instead quietly ask God for his wisdom and help, we put him in his rightful place as the FIRST Parent.

If it helps, picture yourself in the Garden of Eden with God, visibly right there with you and ready to give his advice, love, encouragement, and help. Adam and Eve bought the devil's lie that they could figure it all out for themselves. Unlike them, we need to trust that God loves us and our children so much that he will continually offer us his help and wisdom. So ask God for wisdom. He promises to give it freely and without finding fault (James 1:5).

Practical Parenting TIPS  *For Today*

You've probably heard the saying, "Look before you leap." Well, "Pray before you parent" is the best practical way to get into the habit of looking for and receiving God's help. Right in the middle of what you're doing—especially when you're facing a challenge—turn your attention and your thoughts to God, asking him for wisdom and help. The very act of prayer will usually settle you and get you thinking on a more productive track. You'll find that this habit, like any other good one, takes a while to develop. Be patient with yourself and keep at it; it's worth the effort. Perhaps you could put up a sign for yourself that says, "Free Parenting Help—Just a Prayer Away."

CHAPTER 2

Adam's Family:

Giving Your Child a Purpose-Driven Life

*W*e can benefit a great deal from a hugely important parenting lesson that Eve learned, and in just a moment I'd like to consider that lesson. But first I want to jump forward in the Bible and talk about Moses and his mother.

Acts 7:20 records that Moses' mother hid him from bloodthirsty Egyptian officials because he was "no ordinary child." It would seem that, in some way, God showed Moses' mother that heaven had a very special plan for this little baby. Perhaps knowing he had a special purpose gave Moses the strength to make the right choices when it came time to walk out his destiny (Hebrews 11:24–25).

Now hold that thought as we move back to Eve. The fourth chapter of Genesis opens and closes with the birth of a child; both births prompted a statement from Eve. The chapter opens with Cain's birth.

> *Adam lay with his wife Eve, and she became pregnant*
> *and gave birth to Cain. She said, With the help of the*
> *LORD I have brought forth a man.* (Genesis 4:1)

The chapter closes with Seth's birth.

> *Adam lay with his wife again, and she gave birth to a*
> *son and named him Seth, saying, "God has granted me*
> *another child in place of Abel, since Cain killed him."*
> *Seth also had a son, and he named him Enosh. At that*
> *time men began to call on the name of the LORD.*
> (Genesis 4:25–26)

Consider the contrast between Eve's two statements. Although we could read Eve's first statement as a positive comment, here's what *The Expositor's Bible Commentary* has to say:

> *Her words, however, can also be read in a less positive*
> *light: e.g., "I have created a man equally with the Lord"*
> *(Cassuto, p. 196). In this sense Eve's words are taken as*
> *a boast that just as the Lord had created a man, so now*
> *she had created a man.*

The commentary suggests that this is the most probable meaning for Eve's words, especially when viewed in contrast to her statement after Seth's birth. With Cain she said, *"I have brought,"* while with Seth she said, *"God has granted."* Eve used the word "man" to describe Cain, but the word "seed" to describe Seth. The word "seed" is the same term used in Genesis 3:15, where God foretells that Eve's offspring ("seed"—prophetically speaking of Christ) will crush the serpent's head. Eve's use of the word "seed" in conjunction with her words "God has granted" strongly indicates that she had finally begun to track God's plan for her children.

What did Eve learn in the many years that passed between

the births of Cain and Seth? The very profound but simple lesson that although God has given us the privilege of having and raising children, *he is the one who gives each one of them life, personality, and a future with him.*

Moses' mother hid him from certain death because she recognized him as "no ordinary child"—she knew that God had a plan for him. It's funny, but when we read about Moses, we sometimes assume that because his mother recognized him as "no ordinary child," most other children must be "ordinary." But from God's perspective, there are no "ordinary"—as in "not special" or "without a purpose"—children. For the sake of his plan for all of us, God went out of his way to show Moses' mother how out-of-the-ordinary her son was; but that does not mean he implied that most other children are ordinary. In Psalm 139 David wrote:

> *For you created my inmost being;*
> *you knit me together in my mother's womb.*
> *I praise you because I am fearfully and wonderfully made;*
> *your works are wonderful,*
> *I know that full well.*
> *My frame was not hidden from you*
> *when I was made in the secret place.*
> *When I was woven together in the depths of the earth,*
> *your eyes saw my unformed body.*
> *All the days ordained for me*
> *were written in your book*
> *before one of them came to be.*
> *How precious to me are your thoughts, O God!*
> *How vast is the sum of them!* (Psalm 139:13–17)

David recognized that God creates us all individually with loving design and purposeful intent, and that he gives each of us a unique mission and destiny.

When we adopt this attitude, we will gladly tell our children how special they are and that God doesn't have accidents or favorites. They were created special and born for a divine purpose.

Many of us ask, "Why am I here?" When we raise our children to believe that they are here through God's love and by his wise design, we fulfill our ultimate role as parents: to introduce them to their Creator and help them walk in God's will for their lives, which brings great glory to God.

When we ground our children with the knowledge that God created them and has a plan for their lives, it strengthens their connection with God and helps them stay on God's track when they get invited to leave it or feel tempted to stray.

I think it's very significant that right after the Bible records Seth's birth (and Eve's obvious attitude adjustment), the chapter ends with these words: *"At that time men began to call on the name of the LORD"* (Genesis 4:26).

Practical Parenting TIPS For Today

When we raise our children, as Eve and Moses' mom did, acknowledging and affirming that they were designed with purpose and that God has a special plan for them, it rings true in their hearts. One mother told me that she made a habit of salting her conversations with her son with statements like, "I can hardly wait to see what great things God has for you to do!" Some parents teach their young children to pray every day to God about his plan for their lives. The only way to find out what that plan is, however, and to walk in it, is for them to seek God and walk with him day by day. As your children grow, seed them with the fact that they're called—but also tell them that to find that purpose they need to "call on the name of the Lord," or seek him and his purpose for their lives.

CHAPTER 3

Noah & Sons Inc., Shipbuilders:

The Family That Builds Together...

"The ark is to be 450 long,
75 feet wide and 45 feet high."
(Genesis 6:15)

*W*e all know the story of Noah and the ark. One particular aspect about this familiar tale has always intrigued me, however. When God called Noah, he included his whole family: his wife (Mrs. Noah, as one of my daughters called her); his three sons; and also his three daughters-in-law. Probably they all "pitched" in to build and waterproof the boat.

Noah didn't become the father of boys until after he turned five hundred, and God didn't call him to the shipbuilding business until sometime after that. The huge boat took its maiden and final voyage in Noah's six hundredth year. No doubt Noah's sons spent a good deal of their lives working on their dad's mega-project for God.

I find the timing of the births of Noah's sons telling. While all of Noah's ancestors had their first sons between the ages of 65 and 187, Noah's boys don't start arriving until after his five hundreth birthday—just in time to start their apprenticeships in shipbuilding.

These three boys of Noah, along with their wives, would have to repopulate the planet after the floodwater receded. They needed proper mentoring, to be taught and protected from the influence of the very wicked world in which they had grown up. And how did God intend to help Noah raise his kids well? What was his plan? Part of it, at least, came down to, "the family who arks together, sticks with God together."

When my children were still quite young, I did a project called *The Singing Bible*, an audio storybook that takes children through the big story of the Bible. While it was no ark, I included my children in the process. They sang solos, sang in the kids' choir, played roles in the dialogue, and even gave input into the original ideas and writing.

Through their involvement in the project, my children not only took huge leaps forward in their Bible knowledge and understanding, they also learned to obey God, work for his kingdom, and see the amazing results. To this day, my children talk about that experience, including the things they learned and the fun they had.

God's call went to Noah alone, but clearly the Lord also wanted Noah to prepare and teach his household to follow God. It fascinates me that the way God instructed Noah to complete his ark-building task dovetailed seamlessly and naturally with his duty to raise God-honoring children.

Later God called Abraham to *"direct his children and his household after him to keep the way of the LORD"* (Genesis 18:19). God had Abraham move to a strange country, circumcise every male in his household, and take Isaac to Mt. Moriah and there sacrifice *"your son, your only son, Isaac, whom you love"* (Genesis 22:2).

Hundreds of years later, Joshua stood in front of the people of Israel and made a commitment for himself and on behalf of his family: *"But as for me and my household, we will serve the LORD"* (Joshua 24:15).

In the New Testament, when a jailer in charge of keeping Paul and Silas in prison saw God fling all of his jail doors wide open, he asked, "What can I do to be saved?" They gave him a bigger answer than he expected:

> *"Believe in the Lord Jesus, and you will be saved— you and your household." Then they spoke the word of the Lord to him and to all the others in his house. At that hour of the night the jailer took them and washed their wounds; then immediately he and all his family were baptized. The jailer brought them into his house and set a meal before them; he was filled with joy because he had come to believe in God—he and his whole family.*
> (Acts 16:31–34)

The jailer had asked only about himself; the answer involved both him and his entire household. So he took Paul and Silas home, undoubtedly told his family what had happened, and then had them all sit down and listen to the apostles. Right after that, the whole family got baptized together.

In our society, family members often stay so busy with their own agendas that precious little time remains to do things as a family. Yet all kinds of studies have shown that families who regularly sit down and eat dinner together, for example, come out way ahead of those who don't. Doing things together as a family will strengthen your relationships, thereby multiplying your influence in your children's lives.

"Arking together," or finding ways to serve God as a family, will not only strengthen your relationships, it will powerfully grow your children's faith.

Chances are God already has incorporated a way of involving your whole household in what he wants *you* to do.

Yes, God sees and uses us as individuals; he had a plan for Noah, Abraham, Joshua, and the jailer—but he created the family and uses us as family units as well. Therefore, his plans for the individuals in the family dovetail with his plan for the family so that the children learn to naturally serve God and others as they serve *with* their parents.

Practical Parenting TIPS *For Today*

If you're already working with your church or a ministry of some sort, look for ways that you can include your whole family. Find ways to volunteer together. Offer your house to be used as a gathering place for Bible studies, children's summer programs, or even church social functions. How about mutually sponsoring a child from a third world country, or getting involved in a Christmas outreach program?

CHAPTER 4

The Father and Mother of Our Faith:

The Joy of Parenting

I love it that the first recorded words of God to humankind are all about the joy of parenting:

> *God blessed them and said to them, "Be fruitful and increase in number."* (Genesis 1:28)

Please notice that not only did God's first recorded message to us concern children, but he stated it as a blessing, not as a burden: *"God BLESSED them and said . . ."*

Recently someone told me of a couple who declared that they had decided not to have children because they enjoyed their freedom too much and wanted to remain selfish about it. Although I admire this couple for recognizing their shortcomings, they have their wires severely crossed. Having children and raising them God's way is not a burden—it's a gift and a blessing from God. If that couple knew what a blessing it could be, they would jump at the chance to have children and thereby enrich their lives. Yes, raising children is a responsibility; every blessing comes with responsibilities. Having a lot of money is a huge responsibility, but who would refuse a million dollars because of selfishness?

Abraham and Sarah did not allow selfishness to come between them and God's blessing. I believe that God told the couple to name their son Isaac, which means "laughter," in order to honor this pair's conviction that Isaac truly was a gift and a blessing from God. Let me explain.

When both Abraham and Sarah heard the Lord say that they would have a son, they responded with laughter. Yes, they laughed in part because they had long before left behind their childbearing years; and Sarah, at least, laughed because of doubt. But another emotion also bubbled under the surface. If someone told you that he was going to give you an all-expenses-paid, month-long vacation anywhere in the world, how would you respond? You might well respond with laughter that said, "Wow! That's just way too great to be true!" Abraham and Sarah felt so overjoyed by the possibility of having a child that they could hardly believe it to be true.

When God had earlier told Abram that he would father a multitude of descendants, as numerous as the stars in the sky, we read, *"Abram believed the LORD, and he credited it to him as righteousness"* (Genesis 15:6). Yet when God repeated the still-unfulfilled promise many years later, we read a different story:

> *Abraham fell face down; he laughed and said to himself, "Will a son be born to a man a hundred years old? Will Sarah bear a child at the age of ninety?"* (Genesis 17:17)

Is this unbelief? The apostle Paul didn't think so, for he wrote,

> *Against all hope, Abraham in hope believed and so became the father of many nations, just as it had been said to him, "So shall your offspring be." **Without weakening in his faith**, he faced the fact that his body was as good as dead—since he was about a hundred years old— and that Sarah's womb was also dead. **Yet he did not waver through unbelief** regarding the promise of God, but was strengthened in his faith and gave glory to God, being fully persuaded that God had power to do what he had promised.*

(Romans 4:18–21, emphasis added)

Scripture does not have the same words of commendation for Sarah, who had a different reaction to the news:

> *So Sarah laughed to herself as she thought, "After I am worn out and my master is old, will I now have this **pleasure**?"* (Genesis 18:12, emphasis added)

Yet here's how Sarah responded when the promise came true:

> *Abraham was a hundred years old when his son Isaac was born to him. Sarah said, "God has brought me laughter, and everyone who hears about this will laugh with me."* (Genesis 21:5–6)

God had turned Sarah's skeptical laugh into joyful laughter!

Abraham and Sarah viewed the birth of Isaac as an awesome and wonderful thing. Throughout the Bible, children are considered to be a gift from God and a blessing to the parents who receive them.

> *Sons are a heritage from the LORD,*
> *children a reward from him.* (Psalm 127:3)

Scripture contains many prayers and songs thanking God for the blessing of children, including those of Sarah, Hannah, and Mary. Mary had heard the stories of Sarah and Hannah and had learned that children are an awesome gift and a blessing.

> *Mary said: "My soul glorifies the Lord and my spirit*
> *rejoices in God my Savior."* (Luke 1:46–47)

If you're waiting for the other shoe to drop, here it comes. Sometimes parenting can seem downright overwhelming. Children need constant care, training, and discipline, and none of us is perfectly up to the task. So at times we feel tempted to consider the gift of children as anything but a blessing. I once heard a mother say to her young teenager (in jest of course), "Watch it, buster! I brought you into this world and I can take you back out again!" That about sums up the way we sometimes feel, doesn't it?

Unfortunately, sometimes it goes beyond having a bad day or a frustrating moment. Many parents firmly believe that parenting is a burden, that children are rebels and mischief-makers, that teenagers and adults don't get along, and that siblings would all but kill each other if left alone. I've heard parents complain that their kids won't listen, won't help, don't care, and are just huge pains in their backsides. When we believe these things, we lower the bar of expectation and learn to live with substandard behavior instead of looking to him for help and solutions and choosing to believe God when he calls children a blessing.

If God gave children to you as a blessing and considers them a blessing, then he's already prepared to give you everything you need to experience them as a blessing.

When we choose to believe what God says about our children being a blessing, we raise the bar and look for ways to resolve conflict, restore relationships, and parent God's way. And eventually we see peace return to our households.

If you feel worn out and at the end of your rope with your children, stop and pray right now. Give your situation to God and ask him for help, wisdom, and workable solutions. Ask him to return the atmosphere of his blessing to your household and children. Once you've done that, start thanking him (and keep doing it daily) for your children, trusting him that he's heard your prayer and that he's turning things around. If you keep reading this book and apply the principles from God's Word, then the ideas that God shows you will begin to work for your family.

Don't expect things to get perfect overnight, but continue to stay focused on God's affirmation that being a parent is a gift and a blessing. Then watch him slowly but surely return the joy of parenting.

And even if our household usually reflects God's blessing, we can still all take a page out of Sarah's book. When things start to slide, remember to check your perspective, laugh, and remind God that he called this whole parenting thing a blessing. Then ask him for the wisdom, grace, and help to cause your experience to match his statement.

Practical Parenting TIPS  *For Today*

To restore a sense of peace and blessing to your home, you may want to call a family meeting and bring everyone into the process. Let them know that you'd like a peaceful, co-operative house where everyone gets along and looks for ways to be helpful and considerate. Ask them, "Would you like that?" and then ask for their ideas and participation.

It really works! The next time things start to go bad in your home, first stop and pray, and then remind everyone of the meeting and ask each person to work together to solve the current crisis.

CHAPTER 5

Low Road Lot:

Learning to Parent on the High Road

*H*ave you ever thought about Lot's story? Not just while you're reading about Abraham; I mean a concentrated read on Lot (Genesis 13, 14, 19). It's a mixed-up but weirdly interesting biography, and quite an important lesson for parents lies hidden among the antics. After you've seen the parental moral of the tale, you'll understand why I've come to affectionately refer to this interesting man as Low Road Lot.

After Lot's parents died, his grandfather, Terah, took him in. When his uncle Abram headed toward Canaan, Lot tagged along. Once in Canaan, the families of both Abraham and Lot started to grow, prospering so immensely that they soon ran out of space and could no longer live together. So his uncle sat him down and, for the sake of family peace, suggested that they split up. Uncle Abe gave Lot the first choice of land, and the young man chose the fertile plain where further prosperity seemed assured.

Yet there was a problem with Lot's choice. A big one. He decided to live among the people of Sodom and Gomorrah, cities known for their wickedness. Before long the trouble started and Abraham needed to bail out his nephew. Some raiding kings decided to plunder the cities of the plain, and they took Lot and his family as part of the plunder. When Abraham found out, he gathered up a small army, attacked the unsuspecting kings, and rescued his relatives.

A really interesting bit to this story adds that when Abraham returned not only with Lot but also with the other captives and plunder from the routed cities, he gave a tithe to God but refused to take anything from the kings whom he had just helped. Why? Because he didn't want those men saying that they made him rich.

After this frightening incident, you might expect Lot to rethink his choice of residence and move back to the suburbs. After all, he'd discovered that life in the plains could be dicey. Besides, Uncle Abe just gave him an object lesson that demonstrated blessings come from serving God, not from pursuing wealth. But no, the next time we hear from Lot, he's actually moved right into the city of Sodom, just when God was about to clean up the place with a little fire and brimstone.

By God's grace, a couple of angels show up to rescue Lot and his family, and the hospitable Lot offers them a place to stay. The wicked men of the city then surround his house and demand that Lot send the two guys out so that they can have sex with them. So what does Lot do? He offers the men his two virgin daughters as substitutes. The men refuse his offer, but before they can force Lot to let them in where the men (angels) were, the angels strike them all blind.

What was Lot thinking?

A little later Lot tries to convince the two city boys who want to marry his daughters to leave with them; but they laugh him off. Only in the nick of time do Lot and his family escape. The angels want to take them to the mountains, but —get this—Lot convinces them to allow him to relocate to a small nearby city. And you know the really sad thing? In the end, even Lot fears to live in that city. He ends up occupying a cave.

Lot's wife, it should be said, never made the trip, because in disobedience to God's clear instructions, she looked back at her burning home and ended up as a pillar of salt. She didn't want to leave, and so got her wish in a way she never imagined. And since the potential mates of Lot's two daughters had stayed behind, it was just Lot and his two girls living in their rocky abode. (Do you think there may have been room for them at Uncle Abraham's place?)

One day Lot's daughters figured out that the family line was about to come to an end, so they cooked up a little plot involving a lot of wine and two side orders of indecency. They got their dad so drunk that he didn't know what was happening, and then got him to sleep with them in order to continue the family line. Their offspring eventually became the Moabite and Ammonite nations, bitter enemies of Israel throughout most of Old Testament history.

Do you see why I refer to the man as Low Road Lot? So far as we know, when given a choice of where to live, he never talked to God about it, as he'd seen his uncle do; apparently he didn't even ask his uncle for advice. After spending some time as living plunder, you'd think he'd have learned his lesson about bad choices—but no, he chose to live in Sodom. When warned about the city's imminent destruction, he hesitated; he didn't want to leave. When his angelic guests seemed in trouble, instead of trusting God to rescue them all, he tried to compromise with what he considered a lesser evil, a mob rape of his young daughters. When the angels told him to flee to the mountains, he again insisted on doing things his own way and stayed in a city in the plain. He consistently chose to do what he wanted to do instead of choosing the right thing. Instead of standing by what he believed no matter what, he found ways of compromising.

And how did all of this affect his parenting? Well, he raised his daughters in a place bursting with wicked people. He was ready to marry them off to two young residents of Sodom who laughed at the idea of God punishing bad behavior.

We see the results in his daughters. When confronted with a problem wanting their dad's family line to continue, did they pray? Did they think to go and rejoin their relative, Abraham, who lived not far away? No. They got Lot drunk, had sexual relations with him, and both girls became pregnant by their own father. They chose the first and easiest solution and not even for a moment did they consider their compromise wrong!

Here's the odd thing. You read all of that and think that Lot just didn't "get it"—and yet Peter calls him "a righteous man" (2 Peter 2:7). How was Lot righteous? He knew the God of Abraham and wanted to avoid wickedness; but his constant compromises took him inevitably to failure.

If we are Christians, righteousness has been freely given to us because of what Jesus did for us. So, like Lot, we are called righteous. But how we act and the decisions we make and how we live in front of our children will all have a potent effect on how our kids turn out.

We're all growing into the big righteousness shoes God has given us to wear, and some of the steps we take can be pretty awkward; but for our children's sake, let's live what we believe, without compromise. Lot's compromising eventually made him so blind that he offered his daughters as a sacrifice to sin. That's what we do every time we teach our children to compromise on God's truth.

I love how God brings things full circle. One of Lot's descendants, a Moabite, became a direct ancestor of Jesus. Yet Ruth the Moabite refused the low road when her Hebrew mother-in-law needed someone. When she gave her heart to God and saw what needed to be done, she did it without compromise, even when she could easily have justified her compromise. She ended up marrying a godly man named Boaz who also refused to compromise his righteousness. You might know of their great-grandson; we call him King David.

Children raised not to compromise on what's right go on to shape the world. Children raised to compromise what's right get shaped by the world.

Practical Parenting
TIPS  *For Today*

When we tell a "little white lie" to avoid trouble, or cheat a bit on our income tax, or watch movies or television shows that perhaps we shouldn't, or miss church again and again, or call in sick when we really aren't, we raise our children to believe that truth and God's way of doing things are necessary only when it suits us.

Regardless of how your parents raised you, or how you've raised your own kids so far, you can reject the foolish compromising and begin a new life for your family, starting right now. It's never too late to do the right thing, especially when you serve a God who loves to bring sweetness out of bitterness.

CHAPTER 6

Hagar the Single Mom:

When Life Hands Your Family Lemons...

*E*very family goes through tough times, and many of us have experienced them in two families: our family of origin and the one we started. How can we lessen the impact on our children of disappointing family and relational histories? I believe God gives us insight into this problem through the plight of Sarah's maidservant, Hagar.

When you first read Hagar's story, you almost can't help but believe that she got a really raw deal. But what marvelous grace God showed her in her grief! I'll summarize the story, but if you haven't read it in a while, I recommend that you take a few moments and read it again (Genesis 16; 21:1–21).

Sarah really wanted to give a son to Abraham, but it just was not happening. In fact, her biological clock told her that it was never going to happen. So, according to generally accepted practices of the day, she suggested that Abraham take her maidservant, Hagar, and produce a child for them through her. Abraham agreed and Hagar got pregnant.

A short while later, after the pregnancy began to show, Hagar began to despise her mistress. So then what? Sarah got mad at Abraham and let him know, loud and clear, that the situation was entirely his fault. Abraham basically said, "Hey, she's your servant; you deal with her." (Which, incidentally, is the ancient way of asking the age-old, guy question: "How is it that the results of implementing *your* idea are suddenly *my* fault?")

Sarah then escalated the whole situation by mistreating Hagar, who ran away. Judging from the direction she headed and remembering that she was an Egyptian, Hagar likely took off for Egypt.

And then God intervened.

An angel appeared to Hagar and told her to go back and submit herself to Sarah. He also told her that she would have a son, that she should call him Ishmael, and that the Lord would increase her descendants so that they became too numerous to count. Hagar obeyed and headed home, where she had a baby and called him Ishmael.

Now fast-forward fourteen years. Isaac is born, weaned, and Abraham throws a big party for him. Sarah happens to see Ishmael making fun of his half-brother, and demands that Abraham send both the teaser and his mother packing. The demand upsets Abraham, but God tells him that he should do it. So Abraham gives the two of them some water and food (that's it) and waves good-bye as they wander into the desert.

When Hagar runs out of water, she sits down to cry. The Bible says she sat about a "bow shot" away from her boy, because she didn't want to watch him die. Suddenly an angel speaks to her from heaven, lets her know that God will take care of them, and that all of the things he had previously promised would come true. Then he shows her where to find some water. The Bible doesn't tell us much more about the exiled pair, except to record that they lived in the desert and God was with them.

I like how the angel started his conversation with Hagar. He asked, "What is the matter, Hagar? Do not be afraid" (Genesis 21:17). Hagar had just been ejected for good, along with a son she didn't ask for, by a mate she never chose, with nothing but a skin of water and a bag of food. Now she found herself in the desert, wandering around with nowhere to go, the water gone and expecting her son to die, and the angel asked, "What is the problem?"

From God's perspective, no matter what we've suffered or what difficult circumstances we face, we can move on from where we are because he's right there with us, ready to love us and fulfill his gracious promises to us.

The two greatest commands are "love God" and "love others." It's wonderful when we partner with God to love others and be loved by them in return. But in order for us to experience the love of others, God has to make us very vulnerable to each other. With sin in the world and in our hearts, the vulnerability that God meant as a blessing can become the very thing that allows us to hurt each other so deeply.

Living and loving in a fallen world can involve a lot of hurt and pain. Nevertheless, God wants us to continue to love others and to allow ourselves to be loved in return. That's why we just can't do without forgiveness. Without it, we close ourselves off from love.

Hagar had been hurt and misused. Through no choice of her own, she became a single mom with an absentee mate and no material resources. Yet God said, in essence, "What's the problem? Your circumstances aren't too big for me. You don't need to worry. I'm here and I'm ready to care for you and your boy and take you both forward in my plan for you."

Hagar got the message. She got up and moved forward. By God's grace, her boy didn't die. God was with him and he prospered.

What makes you think it will be any different for you?

Practical Parenting **TIPS** *For Today*

No matter what you've been through or how you've been hurt, God understands and is ready to pour out his grace on you and take you from here. It's natural to think that, while you might be able to make it through, your children won't recover or will be permanently scarred. God knows that you live in a fallen world and that you sometimes suffer at the hands of others, even from family members. The key is to forgive, leave the past behind, and move forward, trusting in your loving heavenly Father and his loving future for you. When you do that, your children will see how it works, making it possible for them to recover and move on as well. They also will learn what to do in the future when hurt comes knocking on their door.

CHAPTER 7

Sarah's Blended Family:

Your Kids, My Kids

*A*braham and Sarah can teach today's blended families a lot. They didn't start off in life planning or asking for one, but it turned out that way, nonetheless.

Remember that Sarah originally wanted Hagar to bear a child for her and Abraham—sort of an ancient surrogate mother. *"So she said to Abram, 'The LORD has kept me from having children. Go, sleep with my maidservant; **perhaps I can build a family through her.'** Abram agreed to what Sarai said."* (Genesis 16:2, emphasis added)

Yet God made it clear that the child so conceived would be Abraham's and Hagar's, not Abraham's and Sarah's:

> *Then the angel of the LORD told her, "Go back to your mistress and submit to her." The angel added, "I will so increase **your descendants** that they will be too numerous to count." The angel of the LORD also said to her:*

*"You are now with child and you will have a son. **You shall name** him Ishmael, for the LORD has heard of **your misery.** He will be a wild donkey of a man; his hand will be against everyone and everyone's hand against him, and he will live in hostility toward all his brothers."*
(Genesis 16:9–12, emphasis added)

Notice that the angel didn't say that Hagar would bear a son for Sarah, nor did the angel talk about Sarah's descendants. God was clearly letting Hagar know that this was her child. Evidently Hagar let Abraham know what the angel had said, because when the boy was born, Abraham named him Ishmael—the name the angel gave Hagar—and later Sarah referred to Ishmael as Hagar's son.

So Abraham, Sarah, Hagar, Ishmael, and Isaac became a blended family. They would have kept separate tents in Abraham's personal suburb, but they all needed to make life work in a difficult situation. This ancient blended family faced the same kind of conflicts and complications that often confront today's blended families.

The Bible tells us that raw feelings, resentment, jealousy, and conflict often erupted between Hagar and Sarah. Abraham frequently felt torn between two agendas. Sibling rivalry arose, and we see some hints of conflict over parenting styles. Somehow, though, despite the difficulties, they all made it work . . . for about fourteen years.

The family endured many difficult moments, as most in blended situations do. But everything worked out, and even though eventually they all parted company, in the end both families (including the children) received God's blessing.

So what did they do right?

Notice the respect that each player in the story showed for each other's sphere of authority. When Sarah first came to Abraham about Hagar's attitude problem, Abraham acknowledged Hagar as Sarah's maidservant and therefore agreed that she needed to respect and obey her mistress. When Hagar ran away, the angel told her to return and submit to Sarah, which she did. When Hagar returned with news of the angelic visit, Abraham and Sarah submitted to God and acknowledged that Hagar would have a mother's authority over her son from then on. When Sarah took her concerns about Ishmael's mocking to Abraham, he considered her maternal authority and took her complaint to God. When God told Abraham to listen to Sarah and send Hagar and Ishmael away, he did so.

This story gives us an important key to making blended families work: showing respect for each other's sphere of authority. So if a child's dad and mom, both legal guardians, live in two places, both households should do their best to uphold the parental authority of the other. If stepparents are involved in a child's life, but not as a parent, they lack the same kind of authority as that of a biological parent. Still, the children should be required to submit to their authority. Siblings, whether half, whole, or step, should be taught to treat each other with respect.

I realize that many factors shape each situation, but if you ask yourself about what authority each party legitimately (and legally) has, and remind yourself to respect it, then you'll find it easier to discern what to do in your unique situation. Try to remember the important passage from 1 Peter 2:17: *"Show proper respect to everyone."*

I find it interesting that the violation of this principle served

as the flashing neon sign that warned Sarah complete separa-
tion had become necessary. When she saw Ishmael mocking
Isaac, she went to Abraham right away.

> *And she said to Abraham, "Get rid of that slave
> woman and her son, for that slave woman's son will
> never share in the inheritance with my son Isaac."*
> (Genesis 21:10)

Seeing Ishmael mistreat Isaac caused Sarah to fast-forward
to a time when she and Abraham were dead and the inheritance got handed out. She clearly felt that Ishmael wouldn't
accept his little brother as head of the household and would
try to prevent him from inheriting everything from their
father, Abraham. When she saw that Ishmael and Hagar did
not respect Isaac's God-given sphere of authority as her firstborn son, she asked to have them removed.

When you first read the story, it may seem that Sarah requested the exile out of spite; but whatever her reasoning, God confirmed her plan when Abraham talked to him about it.

> *But God said to him, "Do not be so distressed about
> the boy and your maidservant. Listen to whatever Sarah
> tells you, because it is through Isaac that your offspring
> will be reckoned."* (Genesis 21:12)

In other words, God agreed with Sarah's request because
Isaac had to be respected as (and get the inheritance of) the
firstborn.

If your authority as a parent is being sloughed off and not
respected, do everything you can to resist the temptation to
join the war and return fire; if you respond in kind, things will
only get worse. Your children will resign themselves to being

in the middle of the war and will tend to stop listening to both of you. Go out of your way to respect the authority of the other parent involved, even in little things: if he or she has made a point of telling the children that they need to show up on time, let your children know that they need to respect that request; then do everything *you* can to help them be there on time. Let your children know, through word and deed, that a parent's authority is to be respected.

This may seem hard, for example, when your request to not let the children watch certain types of movies gets ignored. The message that you send to your children, however, is far more important than any playback to your ex. Also, through your example and your teaching, your children will eventually see the truth and start to make right choices on their own initiative.

And isn't that really the goal? Your extra efforts on tough days will pay off as you raise godly children who love the Lord, show love and respect to others, and walk faithful lives on their own initiative.

Practical Parenting TIPS *For Today*

Here's a common "disrespect" trap to avoid: children find it harder to honor their parents when you disparage them. By belittling and insulting their other parent or other stepparent, you set a very poor example. So bite your lip and show respect for all the parties involved. Sometimes you have to speak frankly to your child about the unacceptable actions of the other parent; but you can do so by focusing on the difference between right and wrong, not by attacking the person. And all the while you can give the benefit of the doubt to the other parent and stress that none of us is perfect.

CHAPTER 8

Putting Isaac on the Altar:

Teaching Our Children Obedience

Then God said, "Take your son, your only son, Isaac, whom you love, and go to the region of Moriah. Sacrifice him there as a burnt offering on one of the mountains I will tell you about." (Genesis 22:2)

Ouch! Abraham has faithfully obeyed God from the start of the biblical narrative. All he ever wanted, and the thing he talked to God about the most, was a son.

At first he had a servant whom he considered close enough to be an heir—and God said no. Then he had Ishmael, and God told him to send the boy away, even though it grieved him. God promised that Isaac would come and prepared Abraham to be a good father and to raise Isaac well. At this point, Abraham had been nurturing, loving, and pouring into his son for around twelve years.

And now God tells him to sacrifice Isaac as a burnt offering!

The Lord told him to go on a journey of about three days. I cannot imagine the anguish Abraham suffered in those seventy-two hours.

When they had almost reached Moriah, Isaac, who was carrying the wood, asked, *"The fire and wood are here . . . but where is the lamb for the burnt offering?"* (Genesis 22:7).

Although Abraham hadn't informed his son about this detail, nor did he give him a complete answer to his question, eventually he must have done so. And so a very old Abraham tied up his twelve- or thirteen-year-old son and placed him on the altar. Interestingly, the text mentions no struggle of any kind.

When we obey God, even at the expense of giving up what we want and/or cherish, no matter what it costs or how it hurts, we teach our children to do the same. Isaac harbored no doubts regarding his father's love and never saw his father's commitment to God falter or get compromised for his sake. He grew up hearing the stories and seeing firsthand the faithful obedience of his father. When Abraham knew what to do, he did it, without argument or compromise. Through his example, young Isaac felt prepared to do the same, even though it looked as if it would cost him his life.

Sometimes our children appeal to our emotions, pulling the strings that they know are attached to our hearts, asking us to compromise what is wise and sometimes even what is right. The more we allow the compromises, the more we prepare our children to wrestle, argue, and pout their way out of living a life of right action and godly principle. "Oh, please could I watch the movie? I know it has a bad rating, but all of my friends are going, and I'll look bad if I don't. Please, just this once." Or, "I really don't feel like going to church and I don't really have any friends there. I'll do homework instead."

The same principle applies when we allow our children to constantly compromise practical wisdom—allowing them to eat junk food too often, letting them waste their money, letting them mistreat their siblings or a friend, or even neglecting to help out around the house.

The Bible teaches that if we spare the rod we spoil the child (Proverbs 13:24; 22:15; 23:13, 14; 29:15), which basically means that if we don't teach our children how life works and then ensure that they apply and live what they've learned, they will grow up unable to make the hard and right choices. Although the word *rod* can be taken literally, the manner of discipline is less the point than effectively teaching your children to make right choices and live a disciplined life. You can manage that without a rod, and parents who use a rod but miss the point will never teach their children anything beyond, "It's going to hurt if my parents get mad at me."

Our children naturally want to avoid work and discipline; like us, they run toward the fun and easy road. Abraham had obviously done such a good job of helping Isaac learn how to make the right choices instead of the easy ones, that by the time Isaac had a really tough choice to make, for the love of God, the love of his father, and in respect of what was right, he willingly obeyed.

Do you think Mary recalled this lesson when she watched Jesus, God's only Son, willingly carry the wood of the cross to his own sacrifice?

Practical Parenting
TIPS  *For Today*

Sometimes the hardest thing to do is to not give the quick "No" answer, especially when you feel tired.

When your children want a fair and reasonable compromise that doesn't involve compromising what is right and wise, then move heaven and earth to work with them.

If you feel your heartstrings being pulled for the wrong reasons, however, gently explain why you cannot compromise, and then DON'T give in. Talk to your child (without allowing him or her to manipulate your decision) and explain why your decision is the best choice for the situation. Your model in making right choices, no matter how difficult, will provide a lesson that will serve your children for a lifetime.

CHAPTER 9

Soft-Hearted Isaac, Part 1:

Teaching Your Children How to Love

*O*ut of all of the patriarchs, Isaac seems to be the quiet and steady one. His biography seems uneventful, compared to the others. When you peruse what the Bible does record about him, however, something jumps out at you again and again: Isaac seemed to get along well with nearly everyone.

First, recall the very close relationship Isaac had with his father. Isaac was the apple of Abraham's eye, and judging from the record, Isaac had a deep love and respect for his father.

We also see hints of Isaac's heart for people in the beautiful story of how he and his wife, Rebekah, got together (Genesis 24). The narrative makes it clear that Abraham's servant had a close relationship with, and a deep respect for, Isaac; but the really telling part of the story occurs right at the end of the chapter.

> *Isaac brought her into the tent of his mother Sarah,*
> *and he married Rebekah. So she became his wife, and he*
> *loved her; and Isaac was comforted after his mother's*
> *death.* (Genesis 24:67)

Isaac and his mother shared a strong bond, so much so that her death still rattled him three years after she died. His tender feelings for his wife are summed up simply with the powerful words, *"and he loved her."* I love those words. It is as if the author felt that nothing else needed to be added. Unusual among the patriarchs, Isaac had only one wife, and he did not hesitate to openly show his affection for her:

> *When Isaac had been there a long time, Abimelech*
> *king of the Philistines looked down from a window and*
> *saw Isaac caressing his wife Rebekah.* (Genesis 26:8)

Also, when Isaac started to greatly prosper and control more land, his neighbors started disputes over water rights. Isaac didn't start fighting; he did that only as a last resort. Instead, he moved on and dug other wells until he found peace with his neighbors.

Isaac had been loved deeply, and apparently he had learned from his parents how to love others both emotionally and practically. Thus he anticipated Jesus statement that the two greatest commandments are to love God and to love others.

Whatever God tells us is for our own good. Therefore, the two greatest commands reflect the two greatest blessings in life: to have a growing, loving relationship with God and to have growing and loving relationships with others. As parents who love our children, these two commands should focus our parenting efforts.

As we've already discussed, helping our children develop a relationship with God is more complex than just reminding them to say their prayers. In the same way, teaching them to love others requires more hands-on, practical training than shouting, "Would you *please* get along!" The Bible doesn't stop at telling us to love; it shows us how. The Bible is full of teaching on relational skills, including everything from how to listen to others and how to settle conflicts, to instruction on putting others' interests before your own, how to cooperate, and how specific relationships (such as friendships, marriages, and boss/employee relationships) should function.

Most people believe that sibling rivalry, family fallouts, teenagers not getting along with their parents, and troubled and broken relationships in general, are all just facts of life. But they are not facts of life; they are often merely the result of poor relational skills. When we don't take the time to teach our children relational dynamics and train them to use them, they don't know how to get along with each other. That's why they argue and fight. Then, when they get old enough to disagree with their parents, they fight with them as well, because they know no other way.

When these kids get married and can't get along with each other after the honeymoon glow disappears, we wonder what went wrong. But why wonder? They've never been taught *how*!

The Christian home should be a classroom for teaching our children how to love in very practical ways. Parent/child relationships should help children learn how to get along with their elders, to work and live in relationships where authority is involved, such as with an employer, to work in leadership roles, and to learn how to relate to their own children one day. Their siblings and friends should provide each child with his or her first opportunity for successful peer relationships and prepare them for relationships with friends, coworkers, and eventually a spouse. The apostle John wrote:

> *If anyone says, "I love God," yet hates his brother, he is a liar. For anyone who does not love his brother, whom he has seen, cannot love God, whom he has not seen.* (1 John 4:20)

John outlined a simple relational principle here: if you can't function well in your human relationships, then you're fooling yourself if you think you have a great relationship with God. The relational principles it takes to build and sustain sacrificial, committed love remain the same in *every* relationship.

Children who don't receive training on how to get along often think they fight with their siblings because they have stupid or uncooperative siblings. After all, they have no trouble getting along with their friends! They don't live with their friends, however, and therefore they have far fewer opportunities for disputes. The same is true when they start to have difficulties with their parents—they tend to think that they somehow got parents from down under (and I don't mean Australia). The truth is, if they can't get along with their family members, then they don't have what it takes to get along with anyone in close quarters over an extended period—and that includes their future spouse and future employer.

Isaac's story shows consistency. He got along with everybody, even the neighbors who desperately wanted to cause trouble for him and with him. Isaac didn't have siblings, but an only child often spends more time with friends and children in community, and the peer relational training either happens or doesn't happen there. When we train our children to love at home and in their community, we equip them to function successfully in every other relationship for all of their lives. Isaac, who would take over as the leader of a clan destined to be a nation, was clearly loved and taught how to love—get along with others and resolve conflict.

When I first discovered this principle, I got my children together and explained it to them. I let them know that I intended to teach them how to love and get along with others. Despite their youth, I began teaching and training them how to get along. If a fight broke out between siblings or friends or cousins over who got to play with a toy or choose the video, I would calmly show them how they could solve the problem themselves by sharing or taking turns. As the occasions arose, I simply taught them how to cooperate and interact with myself, guests, relatives, babysitters, teachers, etc., just like I would show them the right way to throw a ball. After they had been taught how to talk respectfully, share, take turns, listen, hug, help, use kind words, be patient, respect others, pay heed to authority, etc., it took only a gentle reminder to help them settle a dispute or get along properly in any setting. In the next chapter, we'll cover some practical "how to's" for making this work in your home, one step at a time.

Today, my children are the best of friends. They cooperate, spend time together, and calmly work out any potential conflicts. Their lives are full of *great* relationships. The best thing about this isn't merely the peace that has descended upon our home; it's watching them get along in every other relationship—and knowing that, like Isaac, they have the skills to live and love well.

Practical Parenting
TIPS  *For Today*

Get your children involved. Sit your children down and talk to them about this, letting them know that you are going to teach them how to love and get along with others, a skill that will help them enjoy a much better life. Get them on board so that later, when they decide that they don't want to love and cooperate, you can remind them that you all agreed to work together at this. Read 1 John 4:19–21 and discuss it with them.

Soft-Hearted Isaac, Part 2:

Teaching Your Child How to Get Along with Others

*T*eaching your kids practical ways to love and get along with others pays huge dividends. After I discovered this parenting concept in God's Word, I began applying it to my own family. That one phrase about Isaac's people-centered life—*"and he loved her"*(Genesis 24:67)—stayed with me. As I sought to build this principle into the lives of my kids, I started getting great results. Ultimately, my kids learned wonderful relational skills that benefit them to this day.

But you know what? When I tell this story, some people look at me as if I'm from another planet. We have grown so accustomed to children *not* getting along, to family blowups, teenage rebellion, and all sorts of broken relationships, that when we hear a story like this, we consider it just a pipe dream. One person accused me of trying too hard to be a perfect dad; another told me that I didn't have a family, but a social science experiment.

The truth is, I have no special abilities as a dad and I'm as far from perfect as anyone. I merely obeyed God's gentle nudging and relied on his help. As the occasions arose, I gave my children "how to get along" lessons, and eventually they learned how relationships work. It's no different than teaching them how to cook, swim, or apply themselves to their school work. Children will learn what we consistently teach and train them to do; so if you want loving, peaceful children who cooperate and get along well with each other and others, then you need to start showing them how to manage it.

The Bible calls us to love others, but if we don't listen to sound biblical teaching and/or study it for ourselves and learn how to forgive, give, put others first, listen, help when someone is in need, respect the rights and opinions of others, admit when we're wrong, etc., we'll never successfully and practically love anyone. Love isn't a warm and fuzzy; it's something we do. And in order to do it well, we need to learn how and grow in it. The same goes for our children, and we have been given the responsibility to teach and train them how to love.

Allow me to suggest a few simple tips to get you started:

1. *Teach respect for property and person.* Teach your children that each of them is in charge of their own bodies and belongings, and that everyone else is in charge of their own. Teach them that no one can touch them or their things without their permission; they like that. Once you have them nodding their heads, let them know that their brothers and sisters have the same rights. "Just as no one can hit or hurt you, so you can't hit or hurt anyone else." Once you've got them here, take it further. "No one should be able to tickle you, wrestle with you, or tease you against your will." They like that too. Now say that the same

holds true when your brother or sister, friend or cousin wants *you* to stop tickling, wrestling, or teasing. Incorporate a "time-out" so that your children know when someone is calling them to cease. I used the phrase, "Please stop." When one of my children used that phrase, whoever was doing the tickling (or whatever else) understood that they had to stop immediately. It's easy to transfer this same teaching to belongings. No one can touch, borrow, or use something belonging to you without your permission—and others have the same right.

2. *Teach the golden rule.* As you've guessed, the previous rule can be taken too far. For instance, your children may use the rule to keep a tight hold on themselves and all of their belongings. That's where the golden rule ("Do unto others as you would have them do unto you") must be applied. Explain that if they use this rule so strongly that they can never be touched or have others play with their things, then *they* must never touch anyone or play with their things. Teach them that God owns everything and that he wants us to share those things and use them to make others happy. Using the logic of the golden rule backwards is an effective tool, because often children don't see that they would not like getting what they are dishing out.

3. *Teach them how to get along with Mom and Dad.* Once children understand that everyone has clear authority in peer relationships over themselves and their belongings, you can help them understand how it works in authoritative relationships. Explain that even though they have command over themselves, God has given you command over them in order to help them, teach them, and prepare them for life. If you used the time-out signal, "Please stop," for their peer relationships, you can use the same one in your relationship with them. Explain that just as others must stop when they say, "Please stop," so they also need to immediately stop when you say, "Please stop," since you're in charge of them. As your children grow up, remember that you are preparing them to get along with their future bosses, church

leadership, and government officials, etc. Therefore, take them beyond blind obedience to being able to respectfully talk to you about your requests and decisions; as they mature, they can even respectfully disagree. Help them think through their own ideas and issues and talk to you about them, but also teach them to consider your ideas and needs and, of course, to maintain love, mutual respect, and caring in all of your interactions.

4. *Always show them the better way and let them work it out.* When your children start scrapping with siblings or friends over a toy or screaming at each other, or they act disrespectfully to you, don't lose your cool or work it out for them. Go to them, get them settled down, and remind them of the family agreement to learn how to love each other. If it's a peer problem, ask what happened and have each child calmly state his or her case. Then show both of them (not just one, even if one was more in the wrong; children also need to know how to react well to being wronged) what they could have done to resolve the situation peacefully. No matter who created the problem, make sure that they understand how they could have done it right, and then have them redo the situation with the right responses. After you've done this consistently, you'll be able to catch a situation before it escalates; then you can merely remind them to do it the right way. Treat each situation as a training session, and don't think of yourself as constantly rescuing, punishing, or correcting. They've agreed in the family meeting to learn and be trained, so all you have to do is work along with them much more effectively than the "you against them" approach.

5. *Make kindness the rule for everything.* Write or print out the first part of 1 Corinthians 13:4 and put it on your fridge: *"Love is patient, love is kind."* (You might want to put up verses 4–7 and point to whichever verse applies at the time.) If love is kind, then we are to be kind with our words and actions. Discuss this verse with your children and decide together to be kind to one

another. Explain that kindness in speech involves motivation, the actual words, and the tone. Talk about how much better we feel when people treat us with kindness, and help them to understand that life and relationships work much better for us when we are always kind. Even disagreements can be worked out more quickly and easily if we use kindness in the process and were more apt to get what we want! Once they understand, start coaching with every opportunity. If one of your children starts to be unkind, again go to where they are and help them see how they can handle the situation differently remembering to do your own teaching and training with kindness. Also, be sure to allow your children to respectfully point out if you are being unkind; this is, after all, a family commitment.

6. *Adopt the "Cooperative Family" title.* Explain in your original family meeting that families who cooperate with each other tend to be happier. Use examples to show how this works, starting with how they benefit. If your children ask if they can have a friend over, prepare a special dessert that they haven't had for a while, or stay up a little later to watch a very special show, the cooperative thing to do is to strongly consider their request. And if it's not bad for them, then cooperate by agreeing; they'll like that. Then explain that cooperation has two sides. If you ask them to do something—for example, clear off the table—the cooperative thing to do would be to willingly do it. I love this one because once the "we are a cooperative family" tag has been placed, each time one of your children tries to be uncooperative, you can say, "Oh, I thought we were cooperating? If not, I guess I can say no and not drive you to soccer and not give you the money you asked for and not wash your laundry by the morning and . . ." You can say it with a smile on your face, and they'll get the picture and respond. This really helps them to see that relationships are two-sided and that if we want something out of it, we have to put things into it.

7, 8, 9, 10, 11, etc. *Teach them to forgive, teach them to listen in conversation, teach them to be helpful and generous, teach them to put the needs of others ahead of their own, teach them how to compromise and share, etc., etc.* If you demonstrate it, teach it and spend the time training your children how to practically do it right when life is happening, they'll grow up not knowing merely that they should love, but knowing how. Perhaps when your son gets married and someone says, "and he loved her," like the Bible does about Isaac, you'll know that observers have recognized something in your son that goes way beyond a fuzzy feeling and a dumb grin, to something that will last.

Practical Parenting TIPS *For Today*

Once you've had the family meeting and started down this road, it seems to take care of itself, like getting a siphon started. Much of the battle is making the change from constantly trying to get them to get along, to you training them to do it with practical, easy-to-follow steps.

Once everyone understands, accepts, and gets used to the new approach, it's very easy to step into the system each time the need arises. It gets even easier each time you train them in an area, because after you've covered, for example, alternatives to fighting over the remote, all you have to do when things start going sideways is to give a gentle reminder. Don't even think about all you're going to have to teach; and whatever you do, don't try and teach it to your kids at once in some kind of home seminar. Just pray and start your "social science experiment" today and let life's situations provide you a classroom, one opportunity at a time.

CHAPTER 11

Twin Troubles:

Teaching Your Children What Life Is About

*The babies jostled each other within her, and she said,
"Why is this happening to me?" So she went to inquire
of the Lord.* (Genesis 25:22)

*L*ike any young mother-to-be, Rebekah would have seen
and heard of many normal pregnancies—and she knew that
hers was getting weird. Jacob and Esau were struggling with
each other so much that she thought something had gone
wrong. God showed Rebekah that the struggle inside of her
foreshadowed how the two peoples that would descend from
these boys would struggle with one another.

From a New Testament vantage point, we also know that it
represents a spiritual struggle.

*See that no one is sexually immoral, or is godless like
Esau, who for a single meal sold his inheritance rights as
the oldest son.* (Hebrews 12:16)

Esau sold his birthright for a bowl of stew and later got

tricked out of his blessing as the firstborn. The Bible declares that Esau despised his birthright; and when it came to losing the blessing, he lamented only the loss of authority and blessing that he could have received.

Esau completely missed the main point. At the end of the story, we see both Jacob and Esau blessed with family, influence, and material goods; but only Jacob saw that God's blessing surpassed anything that this world can offer.

While God blessed their grandfather Abraham in this world, Abraham didn't live for worldly things.

> *For he was looking forward to the city with foundations, whose architect and builder is God.*
> (Hebrews 11:10)

Every Christian must contend with the struggle that Jacob and Esau's fight represents, and every Christian parent should prepare his or her children for it.

God created us to live in his blessings. He gifted some of us so that we could have a wonderful career that would contribute to society. He wants to bless most of us with a spouse, a happy marriage, and wonderful children. He wants to get close to all of us, teach us, direct us, and shower his grace and love on us. Everything inside us resonates with these truths.

Our world fell into sin, however, and today God has called us to participate in his plan of redemption. Our mission is to help as many people as possible to escape the kingdom of darkness and put down deep roots in the kingdom of light.

These two ideals often seem to conflict with one another.

Our desire to be blessed by God and have a peaceful, successful, and wonderful life appears to conflict with our time in history and what God calls us to do.

Nehemiah experienced this struggle when God called him to help his people rebuild the walls of Jerusalem. Almost immediately upon his arrival in the ruined city, he ran into stiff opposition. What he did about it reveals another picture of this struggle.

> *Those who carried materials did their work with one hand and held a weapon in the other, and each of the builders wore his sword at his side as he worked.*

(Nehemiah 4:17–18)

God wants us and our children to receive his blessings and to build successful lives with his help and guidance—but he also wants us to fight in the spiritual war, advancing his kingdom.

Like the twins in Rebekah's womb, each of our children will struggle to find the balance between succeeding in this life and serving Christ with a whole heart. It's up to us to explain the struggle and then to help them find the balance.

And just how do we do that? Let's look at how Isaac and Rebekah handled it.

Jacob had a close relationship with his mother, while Esau was close to his father. God told Rebekah that Jacob would take Esau's place as the firstborn; she evidently valued the prophecy and taught Jacob to go after God's blessing.

Isaac wanted to bless his son Esau as the firstborn, so either he didn't believe what his wife reported to him about what

God had said, or he no longer cared. It seems that Isaac, like Esau, had become too focused on the here and now. Esau sold his birthright for a bowl of stew; Isaac wanted a meal from Esau before he would bless him. Some commentators believe that the author of Genesis meant to subtly convey this message by the parallel accounts.

So it seems that Isaac and Rebekah got involved in the struggle, each one pulling in the opposite direction. Isaac was more concerned with the blessings of the here and now; and Rebekah sought God's direction for her children's lives. But even though Jacob and Rebekah had focused on God's promise and sought his blessing, they compromised principles of godly living to get it. They plotted, lied, and deceived to get what they wanted—and that, of course, really messed things up.

I believe that we can learn three very practical lessons from this story that will help us to relay a balance to our children. We find the same three points packed into one of Jesus' most famous statements:

> *"But seek first his kingdom and his righteousness, and all these things will be given to you as well."*
> (Matthew 6:33)

It's not an either/or choice; in this verse Jesus mentions both kingdom-building and day-to-day life. We don't need to pull our children toward one and away from another, as Isaac and Rebekah appeared to do. Teach your children that God knows and understands the struggle. He created all of the wonderful things in life and put within us a desire to receive his blessing and to live a happy, productive life. The same God has called each one of us in the body of Christ to help further his kingdom.

We don't have to choose between following God and missing out on life, or ignoring God and having one. If we give our children that faulty idea, it becomes very difficult for them to choose well. God knows how, in each of our lives, the balance can be found and the struggle settled.

It's a matter of priority: teach your children that seeking his kingdom isn't just about building it, but also about studying it, growing closer to God, and maturing as Christians. God wants us to learn to trust him completely and to follow his direction for our lives. When we trust him and know how to follow him, we end up finding his best for our lives and that best will be balanced. Both Jacob and Esau could have found God's best by seeking God first and trusting him to look after them.

The end never justifies the means. Jacob compromised and did wrong to get what he thought was right, but Jesus also told us to seek righteousness. Sin and compromise will take you away from God and his plan. Repentance will put you back on track, but why get off in the first place?

Encourage your children to ask God to help them seek his kingdom and his righteousness first, and to thank him that he'll look after their lives as they do so. Tell them stories of how you've prayed and trusted God for direction and how things worked out for you. Let your children in on your decision-making process; show them how you put God first and ask for his wisdom and leading. Let your children see you enjoy God's blessings in life and invite them to watch as you live this life with eternal life in mind.

Practical Parenting
TIPS
For Today

Teach your children that the easiest and most basic way to follow God is to always choose right over wrong. A small compromise may not, at the time, seem like a big deal; but each one we make takes us on a detour off God's road for us. Jacob and Esau made bad choices and went through a lot of grief because of them. God uses our right choices to build our faith for eternal life and to appreciate all he has blessed us with on this earth.

CHAPTER 12

Rebekah's Not-So-Wise Words:

Giving Your Children Advice

*W*hen Rebekah heard that her beloved and mostly blind husband was about to give the blessing of the firstborn to Esau—despite God's word to her that the blessing was to go to Jacob—she hatched one of the most unbelievable plots in the Book of Genesis.

Jacob wasn't hairy like his brother, so she had him dress up in his brother's best clothes and strap on some goat skins to make his skin feel more like his brothers. Then she told him to lie and say he was Esau in order to take the blessing by stealth and deception.

It brings to mind another crazy Bible story about Balaam and his talking donkey. (You thought that was a *Shrek* original?) The Moabites tried to hire Balaam to curse the Israelites.

Balaam warned them that he could speak only the words God gave him. Although Balaam wanted the reward money and the Bible doesn't at all paint him as a godly man, he just could not get a curse out of his mouth. Three times he tried to curse Israel, and three times he ended up blessing them instead.

I recall the story because if God said that *Jacob* was to get the blessing, then he would get it. He didn't need Rebekah's deceit and bad advice to get the job done. If God had so chosen, he could easily have changed the words as they came out of Isaac's mouth.

We need to be careful what advice we give to our children. Sometimes as kids we didn't get the best of advice, and in the heat of the moment, we pass on the bad counsel we received. Before she moved away to marry Isaac, Rebekah had lived with her older brother, Laban, and Laban was a very deceitful man.

We chuckle when we think of advice like, "Don't make faces or your face could get stuck that way," and I hope we say such things only for a laugh and then follow it up with the truth. If we present as truth old wives' tales, fairy tales, or things that we're just not sure about, however, we run roughshod over a very important God-given responsibility: to teach our children to build their lives on truth.

When your son tells you how a school bully picks on him and your emotions begin to run wild, you can easily feel tempted to pass on bad advice you heard as a kid about relying on violence to resolve such a problem. Catch yourself, and think and pray about it first, for at least two reasons: if it's not God's way, ultimately it will cause more trouble; and the more often you hand out ungodly advice, the harder you make it for your children to listen to your good advice.

I've learned the hard way that the more I keep my opinions to myself and stick to telling my children what the Bible says, the more they listen to my advice, understand it, and heed it. I remember trying desperately to explain a life principle to my then three-year-old daughter, simplifying it as much as I could; but she just did not understand me. Then I thought about just telling her what the Bible said. I almost kept quiet, because I reasoned that if she couldn't understand my simplifications, she certainly wouldn't understand the Bible verse. But at the end of my rope, I tried it. I barely got the verse and a short explanation out of my mouth before she began to smile. She understood, explained it back to me, and then ran off to play. Not since that moment have I ever doubted the power of God's Word to guide and teach my children. It's not always that easy, of course, but I got God's message to me— his wisdom and way of explaining life is better than mine, and his words have the power to get the job done.

Try it out the next time you're attempting to explain something to your children—when that verse pops into your head, go with it. And if you're not sure what the Bible says, take the opportunity to show your child how to use God's instruction book for life and look it up together.

I wonder what might have happened had Rebekah merely repeated to Jacob the promise God had given her, and then affirmed that God was able to keep his promise, even if Jacob wanted to bless Esau? It might have saved them all a lot of grief.

You can give your children wise words of advice . . . God's words. And if you want peace rather than grief in your home, you'll make a habit of it.

Practical Parenting
TIPS  *For Today*

If you're like me, you probably can't grab your Bible and know exactly where to turn to find God's advice whenever some issue or problem arises. When you don't know what the Bible says, or you know basically but don't know where to find the verses, take the opportunity to teach your children how to reference God's instruction manual for wisdom and look it up together. If you don't have any Bible reference books, I suggest that you make a small investment in your children's future and make the purchase. A concordance is a great start (most good study Bibles have a limited one in the back), but Id also recommend *The New International Encyclopedia of Bible Words and/or Naves Topical Bible.* If your children are younger, a good book to start with is *801 Questions Kids Ask about God.* The Internet also has good Bible research sites, such as Biblegateway.com.

Jacob's Mood Toward His Brood:

Playing Favorites

*W*hen we get parented the wrong way, we usually know it by the time we reach adulthood. And once we become parents ourselves, we have two choices: think and pray things through and do a little reading and seek some good advice; or default to repeating the mistakes of our parents.

Jacob, unfortunately, ended up repeating the mistake of his father, Isaac. Isaac showed favoritism toward Esau; and instead of thinking this through and remembering what he went through, Jacob played the same game with his kids.

(Just an aside: The fact that parenting mistakes often get passed down the generational ladder is reason enough for us to go to our children when we've blown it, ask for their forgiveness, and then show them how it *should* be done. We may think that we save face by not mentioning our mistakes, but if we see our children make those same mistakes with our grandchildren, we'll feel the shame anew and amplified. And now back to our regularly scheduled program.)

Jacob's father-in-law complicated matters by tricking him into marrying Leah as well as her younger sister, Rachel, whom Jacob had already agreed to marry. He had fallen madly in love with Rachel, not with Leah. That, combined with the example set by his parents, and the fact that Rachel gave birth to Joseph and Benjamin in his old age, caused him to favor Rachel's sons.

Joseph became the not-so-lucky son who received his father's most blatant favoritism, which, of course, sparked jealousy and hatred in his brothers. That led to the infamous event in which Joseph's brothers sold him as a slave and suggested to their elderly father that wild animals had killed him.

But Jacob apparently didn't stop with favoring Rachel's children; he prioritized his children as if he were separating his good goats from his better goats, or like he was grading meat.

When Jacob returned home after twenty years away from his family, he feared for everyone's lives when his estranged brother, Esau, came out to meet him with four hundred men. So he put the maidservants, and the children he had by them, in the front, in harm's way. Then he put his not-so-favored wife, Leah, and her kids next; and finally he put Rachel and her children in the back, a long way from trouble (Genesis 33:1–2). Can you imagine not only how the women felt—but how the children must have felt?

We need to base our actions and attitudes toward our children on an unchanging love—not on shifting emotions. It's normal, at times, to feel more of a pull toward the one most like us, or sometimes to the one most unlike us, or perhaps to the one accomplishing the most, or sometimes to the one who gives us the least grief. If we recognize that these feelings change based on changing circumstances, then we can work to make sure that we demonstrate an even love toward them all.

If you have stepchildren, realize that it's natural to feel closer to your own—but again, if you base your actions on committed love and not on your fluctuating emotions, then you will be able to treat all of those under your roof (or in the larger blended family) with the same kind of love and favor. Jacob became guilty of favoritism and damaged his family when he acted on his emotions and chose to treat some of his children better than the others.

It's interesting to note that Joseph, after suffering so much because of his brothers' jealousy, did not seem to want favoritism to mark his own family.

> When Joseph saw his father placing his right hand on Ephraim's head he was displeased; so he took hold of his father's hand to move it from Ephraim's head to Manasseh's head. Joseph said to him, "No, my father, this one is the firstborn; put your right hand on his head." (Genesis 48:17–18)

When Joseph saw his dad begin to honor the younger son over the firstborn—as he had experienced—he immediately jumped in and called foul. He calmed down only when Jacob told him that he did it because God had showed him something about the future—not favoritism, but calling.

God built each of our children uniquely; everyone has different strengths, will experience different trials, and is called to different futures. But each one equally deserves our unchanging love and commitment through good times and bad, and through the unpredictable changes of our ever-so-fickle emotions.

Practical Parenting
TIPS *For Today*

In order to practically show that you love all of the children evenly, you must make an effort to treat them fairly. If you come into a room and hug one child or ask them how their day went, be sure to do the same with any other children in the room. Also, be careful of unevenly dishing out "special little parental blessings"—letting one child sit in the front of the car more often than the others, or buying one a special treat more often. To prevent this from happening, put some simple "fairness" rules in place for your family. Put a "turn schedule" in place for who sits in the front seat with you, and if you buy a treat after soccer practice for one child, either pick up something for those at home, or if everyone has lessons of some sort, make sure they all get a treat after their lesson. Whatever you do, don't lighten up on demonstrating your love to the ones for whom you currently have a warm and fuzzy feeling; use them as the standard love level, and boost your efforts to all the others to match it.

CHAPTER 14

Jacob's Twelve:

Dealing with Testosterone

*I*t amazes me how many parenting stereotypes there are. It's even more amazing how we tend to quote them as platitudes when we don't know what else to do.

A friend I grew up with could tell you about the time he knocked a kid off a fence with a slug to the head. A short while later, the boy's mother showed up with her bruised-up boy in tow. My friend cowered and wondered what punishment would befall him as he heard the plaintiff state her case. He felt very, very relieved when his mother calmly stated in his defense, "Well, boys will be boys."

It's a good thing Jacob didn't respond with such a statement to his own sons' antics. When their sister got raped, the family of the offending young man offered restitution and marriage. While Jacob tried to work things out, his boys worked on a plan of their own. They insisted that before a marriage could take place, all the men of the city would have to be circumcised. The unsuspecting citizens went along with it, which appears to demonstrate how far they would go to make things right. While the men were still incapacitated, Simeon and Levi killed all of them, and then the rest of Jacob's sons joined their brothers to loot the city and carry off everything, including the women and children.

Boys will be boys? No. Jacob rebuked them harshly. Many years later, just before he died, he said this about the two perpetrators:

> *"Simeon and Levi are brothers—their swords are weapons of violence. Let me not enter their council, let me not join their assembly, for they have killed men in their anger and hamstrung oxen as they pleased. Cursed be their anger, so fierce, and their fury, so cruel! I will scatter them in Jacob and disperse them in Israel."*
> (Genesis 49:57)

I find it interesting that Jacob, while speaking under the Spirit's influence, outlined for us what we need to teach our boys. Let's go through it.

"Simeon and Levi are brothers."

First, note that God lumps the two boys together. They plotted together, encouraged one another, and acted together. It is important that we guide and help our boys in the matter of choosing their friends. Teach them that we become who we hang out with (Proverbs 13:20), and that although we can have many friends, we should choose to spend time with the ones who love God so that they can influence each other for good.

"Their swords are weapons of violence."

The Bible doesn't condemn having a sword, but it does forbid using it as a weapon of violence. Law enforcement, justice, and even self-defense are all biblical concepts. Romans 13:1–7 teaches that governments, soldiers, police, judges, etc.—and the force they use to subdue wrongdoers—are all part of God's system of justice.

And what are we to make of Jesus' famous quote about getting a smack upside the head? *"If someone strikes you on one cheek,"* he said, *"turn to him the other also"* (Luke 6:29).

Jesus intended to warn us against taking up an offense or seeking retaliation, and to encourage us to love the offender, which makes us vulnerable to another smack. The Bible records a time when Jesus got smacked in the face. Far from being passive about it, he stood up and denounced what the guard had done. He did not, however, seek retaliation: *"If I said something wrong,"* Jesus replied, *"testify as to what is wrong. But if I spoke the truth, why did you strike me?"* (John 18:23).

"Let me not enter their council, let me not join their assembly."

We should not listen to those who counsel revenge or violence, nor should we join with them or hang out with them. Obviously, one of Jacob's sons influenced the rest with his bad idea. Teach your boys that the best way to avoid trouble is to stay away from where it's about to happen. As soon as they hear other boys talking about fighting, revenge, or violence, it's time to leave. This seems obvious, but if we don't regularly encourage our boys to make these kinds of decisions, small compromises can sneak in . . . and small compromises can lead to increasingly larger ones.

"For they have killed men in their anger."

It's imperative that we teach our boys what anger is and what they need to do with it. The Bible says, *"In your anger do not sin"* (Ephesians 4:26). It doesn't say, "Do not be angry." Emotions are signals designed to help us determine when something is wrong and/or right. They also motivate us to do something about it. God gave us the emotion of anger to help us recognize injustice and to motivate us to seek solutions to problems. Sometimes we become angry when we shouldn't, or we become angry at the wrong thing or the wrong person. We need to teach our boys to recognize anger and then think through why they feel that way and what the right course of action might be. That's being angry without sinning. When we lash out and act in anger without thinking and/or without considering right and wrong, we sin.

"And hamstrung oxen as they pleased."

Okay, many guys like to tell unkind jokes about cats; but if you do, make sure your sons know they are only jokes. When God gave us animals to eat, he warned us that we must treat them well. We need to instill in our sons a respect for all life. When they start pulling the legs off insects, that's when we need to step in and help them to respect life. Of course, there's a balance. If some creature endangers your life, family, home, or livelihood, and the only recourse is to kill it, then it must be done. But someone who respects life will not do so with pleasure.

"Cursed be their anger, so fierce, and their fury, so cruel!"

Jacob had in mind a bad temper or rage, not mere anger. Have you ever heard a man say he was so mad he saw red, or justify his offense by saying how mad he was? Again, this is an incorrect use of God-given anger. We are to use wisdom and self-control in everything. Being angry is not a valid excuse for misbehavior. Unfortunately, some consider it manly or tough to express a bad temper or to solve problems or conflicts by flying into a rage. Uncontrolled anger in small children is called temper tantrums. Unchecked, it becomes fierce anger and cruel fury. Teach your boys from the start that this is not how a man acts. Teach them self-control. Raging tempers do not solve conflicts; they complicate them (Proverbs 29:22). Also, even if wronged, a real man should never be cruel, but merciful to the offenders. Mercy can't come from uncontrolled anger (James 1:19–20).

"I will scatter them in Jacob and disperse them in Israel."

As a warning to future generations, God treated their behavior severely. Their descendants *were* scattered and never had a real place in the Promised Land. This kind of behavior has no place in a man's life.

Boys will be boys—and will always remain boys—if they're not taught any better. But boys will be men if they are.

Practical Parenting TIPS *For Today*

Every parent struggles with their son's interest and curiosity in all things rough, tough, and even violent. Wrestling, action films, violent cartoons, swords, toy guns, and super-heroes—they all call out to our boys, and every parent struggles with where to draw the line.

Try your best to explain to your children the difference between the "sword" (law, justice, and self-defense), and a "weapon of violence" (cruelty, revenge, and getting pleasure from seeing others hurt). Help them choose appropriate movies, TV shows, cartoons, books, and video games. Which category do they fall in: "sword" or "weapon of violence"?

Abraham, Isaac, and Jacob:

The Power of the Blessing

$\mathcal{I}$n his book, *Choosing to Live the Blessing,* my friend, Dr. John Trent, describes how a biblical revelation and a personal realization changed his life, his ministry, and his family forever.

In the late '70s, John worked as an intern in a psychiatric hospital and, in his words, *"viewing broken dreams and shattered hearts were part of each shift."*

One day as he prepared to teach a Bible study on the Book of Genesis, he read from chapter 27 about Jacob and Esau and their struggle to get their father's blessing. Esau's heart-wrenching plea jumped off of the pages of his Bible.

> *When Esau heard his father's words, he burst out with a loud and bitter cry and said to his father, "Bless me— me too, my father!"* (Genesis 27:34)

John saw in Esau's words his own lifelong heart-cry. He had sought his father's blessing many times, but it always remained out of reach. Then it hit him: Esau's cry didn't reflect merely his own heartache; it lay at the heart of the life-stories he heard each day in the psychiatric hospital.

We all need to be loved and accepted. God placed these needs at the very core of our beings for the sake of equipping us for a vital, meaningful relationship with Him and with others. And it's through our parents' blessing or approval that we are to learn how to give and receive these blessings.

Yet in this fallen world, many children grow up without these needs being fulfilled; unfortunately, they often end up parenting the same way. That's why so many of us walk around with huge, aching voids in our hearts.

Abraham, Isaac, and Jacob blessed some of their children before they died, but God's plan as stated in Genesis 26:4 called for *"all nations"* to be blessed through Abraham's seed. Thanks to Christ dying for us, each one of us who comes to Christ can be unconditionally loved and accepted by God.

The blessing goes beyond just receiving forgiveness from God, however. Jesus' death didn't only restore our relationship with God; it also gives us the ability to truly love and accept others, through His Spirit who lives in our hearts. Therefore, we can break the "unblessed" cycle and raise children with love and acceptance reservoirs full and overflowing, and then help them to pass on the same abundance to their children.

John Trent breaks down "living the blessing" into five elements:

1. *Meaningful touch.* The patriarchs kissed, put their hands on, and even sat the objects of their blessing on their knees.

2. *A spoken message.* They spoke words of affirmation and encouragement.

3. *Attach high value.* The word *bless* literally means to bow the knee or show honor to the person being blessed. They spoke words that showed the high value they placed on the ones blessed.

4. *Picturing a special future.* The patriarchs spoke prophetically about their children's future. We can do something similar by affirming their gifts, talents, and attributes, and encouraging them in the wonderful future that God has in store for them.

5. *An active commitment.* The patriarchs' blessings didn't end with their words; they actively did what they needed to do to set up their children to be blessed.

In Christ, we are all Abraham's seed and heirs to God's promised blessing. We don't need to wait until we're about to die and then choose a few of our children to bless; we can do it day-in and day-out with each of our children—and in so doing, see a generation raised without the aching void that John Trent recognized in Esau's cry.

Practical Parenting
TIPS  *For Today*

Follow the steps of blessing your child, as outlined above. Do it regularly!
1. Express love through meaningful touch.
2. Give a spoken message of encouragement.
3. Honor by speaking and showing high value.
4. Picture a special future and share it with your child.
5. Make an active commitment to bless your child.

*I highly recommend that you read Dr. John Trent's books. This is just a morsel off his banquet table. *Choosing to Live the Blessing* used by permission.

CHAPTER 16

Mommy and Little Moses:

Teaching Your Toddlers

$\mathcal{D}$on't you just love the way God answers prayer? Moses' mother hid him from the Egyptian soldiers who sought to kill all Hebrew baby boys. After a while, she realized that she just couldn't hide him anymore. So she cooked up a really strange plan to waterproof a basket and float the boy on the Nile. Her plan convinces me that she prayed and was inspired to do what she did, because without God, the idea was just plain nuts.

She put Moses in the river and left his big sister, Miriam, to hide and watch. Along came Pharaoh's daughter, who "just happened" to be out for a stroll and a bath. She found the baby and decided to keep him. Just then big sister popped out and offered to find someone to nurse the baby.

So Moses returned home; his mom didn't need to hide him anymore and she got paid for doing her own day care. Now, *that's* answered prayer!

As he often does, however, God threw a twist at Moses' parents. As an infant the boy was to be nursed and cared for, but then he would be given over to Pharaoh's daughter to be raised and educated in Pharaoh's court.

The Bible doesn't say how long Moses remained at home before he moved to Pharaoh's place. Stephen, in his speech in Acts 7, seems to say that he was only three months old when he left home; but it is likely that Stephen had in mind the age of Moses when he was found in the river and adopted by the princess. After that, Moses would have spent a good deal of time with his mother as she nursed him. According to the *New International Bible Dictionary*, children usually weren't considered weaned until they reached the age of three; some were even older. Whatever the case, Moses' time at home appears to have had a powerful effect on him:

> *By faith Moses, when he had grown up, refused to be known as the son of Pharaoh's daughter. He chose to be mistreated along with the people of God rather than to enjoy the pleasures of sin for a short time. He regarded disgrace for the sake of Christ as of greater value than the treasures of Egypt, because he was looking ahead to his reward.* (Hebrews 11:24–26)

What Moses' parents apparently taught him—about his God, his faith, and his people—before he left home had more of an impact on him than all of the knowledge, splendor, and temptations of Pharaoh's court. It's hard to see how they could have had such a huge impact on a three-month-old child; but on a child who is three to five years old? That's a completely different story.

All kinds of studies have shown that what a child learns in these formative years can have more of an impact than what they learn at any other time in their lives.

You may not have many distinct memories from that period in your life, but what we learn and discover each day gets laid on the foundation of what we've learned up to that point. Therefore, a child taught the framework of truth from birth collates all he learns day by day with that truth, thus continually strengthening the foundation laid in the formative years.

The Book of Proverbs says, *"Train a child in the way he should go, and when he is old he will not turn from it"* (22:6).

By looking at the decisions that Moses made, outlined in the verses on page 89, we can see what topics Moses' parents likely emphasized in their "early learning" sessions. They taught him: who he was (v. 24); right from wrong (v. 25); God's plan (v. 26); a basic framework of God's truth.

Following their lead, we need to teach our toddlers that God made them special, loves them, and has a plan for their lives; the difference between right and wrong and why they should choose right; and God's plan of salvation through his Son, Jesus.

Moses chose what was right because it was right. Lessons in right and wrong shouldn't concentrate on being a good or bad boy, but about making the right choices according to God's Word. If you tell a child that he's bad, he'll believe you. Instead, come alongside your children and train them to do the right thing in every circumstance, just as you potty train them or teach them to feed themselves. When you train them to do the right thing and patiently persist, they'll "get it." They aren't bad if they do it wrong for a while, just as they're not bad because they don't feed themselves perfectly when you first hand them a spoon. Praise them again and again, include God in your instruction, and let them know how pleased he is when they do well. God gave us *good* gifts when he gave us children—they just need to be trained how to live. And that includes doing what's right and not what's wrong.

Further, I recommend that we should teach Jesus' story and what it means to us, to our children as early as they can understand it (which happens before we think it does). Introduce your toddlers to God's salvation plan in the context of his love, his blessings, and eternal life in heaven.

Although it's never too late to start, I believe that we give our children and our own spiritual training efforts a firm foundation and a huge head start when we follow the lead of Moses' parents and *get after it early.*

Practical Parenting TIPS *For Today*

Toddlers learn from logical, emotional, and experiential association. In other words, when your little ones hurt and you respond in a kind, gentle way, reminding them that you care, they learn what caring is. When they hurt, affirm your care, but also affirm God's even greater care by speaking of his love; you can also tenderly pray for them. This helps toddlers realize that God is involved in every aspect of their lives. Make these prayers very brief and simple so that your child understands.

CHAPTER 17

Miriam, Aaron, and Moses:

The Principle of the First Born

$\mathcal{M}$iriam, Aaron, and Moses: what a powerhouse set of siblings! Moses made his mistakes, but at the end of his life he scored high on the "well done, thou good and faithful servant" index. And although we tend to remember Aaron for the whole golden calf thing and Miriam for her little "you're not the boss of me" fit against Moses, the Bible also casts both of Moses' siblings in a very good light (see Exodus 32, Numbers 12).

Miriam was the firstborn; we see her first in Scripture helping her mother look out for her baby brother, Moses. She's pictured as a confident, self-possessed girl who had the wisdom and guts, and perhaps even the sensitivity to God's Spirit, to come out of hiding at the right moment and offer to find a Hebrew woman (her mother) to nurse the newfound Moses for Pharaoh's daughter.

The Scripture records that she heard from God, was a prophetess, and that she eventually became a leader in Israel.

Aaron was Moses' faithful helper from the start. He served as Israel's first high priest. He heard directly from God on at least two occasions, and all of Israel mourned for a month when he died.

How is it those three giants of the faith all came from the same family?

First, unlike many of the complex family situations of the patriarchs, all three children (except for Moses beyond the age of three) were raised by their mom and dad in one house. Second, gauging from what Scripture records, their parents brought them up to serve the God of Abraham, Isaac, and Jacob. In short, they had a family life and structure similar to many families today.

The real significance of this story, I believe, is the "principle of the firstborn." Let me start with getting you to think about the way God created parenting as a progressive responsibility.

I watched when a friend of mine raising two young children married a "free spirited" young woman with no serious responsibilities and who had never had children. My well-off friend owned a large house, so his new wife went from no responsibilities to being a spouse, a full-time mother of two young children, and the keeper of a 6,200-square-foot home. Her first child arrived a little less than a year after the wedding. Sadly, but predictably, the situation and the young wife self-destructed, and eventually the marriage ended.

God in his grace created a nine-month pregnancy in which the responsibility of having a new arrival grows from a little inconvenience to a much larger one. With the arrival of a second baby, the responsibility index rises again. God designed families to grow incrementally so that the parents could grow progressively in their ability to handle the responsibility.

Now let's discuss the biblical concept of mentoring, that the older teaches the younger. Older women teach the younger; men teach young men; and established leaders teach young leaders. The same principle applies in the family, where parents teach the children and older children help teach their younger siblings.

With these foundation stones in place, let me reveal the wonderful principle of the firstborn. In his glorious grace, God gives us more time with (and usually more focused enthusiasm for) teaching our firstborn; and usually where the firstborn goes, the little siblings follow. So if we take advantage of the time and enthusiasm that God gives us with our firstborn, then not only do we train ourselves to be good parents, but our job with the second and third will be easier, because the first sets the example for the others to follow.

Moses' parents evidently poured their time and their faith into their firstborn, Miriam, and reaped the benefits. We see Miriam helping her mother in God's business for their family, getting involved in the project, and being there to witness the miracle that God delivered. By the time Moses' parents had to focus on raising, training, and preparing Moses to live in Pharaoh's palace, they had grown in responsibility, knew what to do, and had two young examples and mentors to help them get the job done.

Moses followed Aaron, who followed Miriam, who must have been taught and trained with time and enthusiasm by her parents. And eventually all three answered God's call . . . and helped each other change the world.

Practical Parenting TIPS *For Today*

The family system as God created it is finely tuned and works well when we work it as he intended. Even now, if you're having trouble with your firstborn, don't ignore it, hoping it'll go away because you're just too busy with the young ones. Stop and find a way—with God's wisdom, the help of others, and/or advice from good parenting books—to solve the problem with your firstborn. In so doing, you'll learn and be able to help the next one through the same thing, and you'll have help from an older sibling who can support you by wisely advising his or her younger siblings.

CHAPTER 18

Moses and Zipporah:
Parenting Together

*W*ith the burning bush still aflame in his memory, Moses reluctantly but obediently headed out to speak the famous "let my people go" line to Pharaoh. Right after he put his wife and sons on a donkey and started back to Egypt, something happened that seems pretty strange.

> *At a lodging place on the way, the LORD met Moses and was about to kill him. But Zipporah took a flint knife, cut off her son's foreskin and touched Moses' feet with it. "Surely you are a bridegroom of blood to me," she said. So the LORD let him alone. (At that time she said "bridegroom of blood," referring to circumcision.*
>
> (Exodus 4:24–26)

No one knows how God threatened Moses' life, but I've read speculations ranging from a debilitating disease to an avenging angel with a sword. One can deduce a few things from the facts of the story given in the Bible. For one, Zipporah had to perform the circumcision (if Moses were able, he would have done it). Second, she did it in order to save Moses' life. It is clear that whatever the threat, it was very real and evident to all.

In reading the details of this event, we can also deduce a very powerful parenting lesson.

First, let me paint the backdrop for the parenting aspect of this story. Moses married Zipporah during his forty years in Midian. The Midianites were descendants of one of Abraham's sons from Keturah, the woman he married after Sarah died (Genesis 25:2). Although it's likely that Zipporah's family believed in the God of Abraham, it's possible that she held a very different view of circumcision; either the Midianites didn't follow the practice at all, or more likely, they performed the surgery when the boys were older. Moses had been taught, however, that God commanded Abraham to circumcise boys when they were eight days old. Further, God said that any uncircumcised male would be cut off from God's people.

Apparently Moses and Zipporah had a disagreement over the issue and, possibly for the sake of peace, Moses chose not to deal with it. ("Thus for one small neglect, apparently out of deference for his wife's wishes, or perhaps to keep peace in the home, Moses almost forfeited his opportunity to serve God and wasted eighty years of preparation and training!" says the *Expositor's Bible Commentary*.)

Do you see the problem here? The guy to whom God chose to give his commandments, and to emphasize the crucial importance of obedience, was about to show up with an uncircumcised son. Moses needed to understand the gravity of his task and the importance of obeying God in everything he did before he could teach others.

So why did Moses make the compromise when he knew better? It appears that he and his wife simply did not agree on the issue. And instead of working together to resolve it, they evidently avoided it . . . until God forced the issue.

I have watched families live in perpetual turmoil because they refused to resolve their differences regarding their parenting approaches. When parents do not agree and don't work to resolve their differences on how to parent, the children don't know what to do and end up playing one parent against the other. Therefore, they don't learn how to cooperate and obey; they learn instead how to get their own way. Families who function this way (or dysfunction this way) have no peace, because every time a child gets out of line, the parents get into strife with each other; and in order to get their own way, the children enter the strife and argue with their parents; and then because strife is the only way they know to handle conflict, the strife extends to the siblings.

In a word, bedlam.

It's hard to live in bedlam; it's almost impossible to go on a road trip with it. After things came to a head on the road to Egypt, Moses continued on and Zipporah and the boys returned to Midian.

It's vitally important, for the sake of the children and for family peace and unity, for parents to agree about their parenting methods and then present a united front to the children. No matter how big your differences, even if you're married to an unbeliever, you can make it work—if you see how important it is and you're willing to work at it.

Set some time aside with your spouse to discuss this issue. If you have trouble agreeing on how you should handle important issues, get a basic parenting book that you agree on, read it together, and follow its instructions together. Or perhaps take a class, or go visit your pastor together, agreeing that you'll find some plan of action that you can follow together.

You can also divide up the parenting responsibilities. If you feel passionate about teaching the children table manners, then take responsibility for that training and let your spouse deal with something else—say, training the children to get along with each other. Once you've agreed who's doing what, don't ever step in when the other person is doing their job, and don't undermine your spouse's authority by doing something different in "their" area when they aren't around.

What should you do if your children try to play you against each other? Agree with your spouse that whoever handled the situation first sets the agenda for how the situation stays handled. When your children ask you something, before you answer, ask them if they've already talked to the other parent. If they have, stick with the answer already given. I would always say, "Your mom and I are a parenting team; what one of us says, we both say." After a while, my children stopped trying this tactic. Again, if you don't like what your spouse said or how they dealt with the issue without consulting you, follow the process anyway and then talk about it later.

I encourage you, and even plead with you: don't let it simmer until it boils over on the proverbial road to Egypt! Do the hard work *now* and do whatever it takes to make it work. You can turn a home torn with bedlam into a home enveloped in harmony if you parent *together.*

Practical Parenting
TIPS
For Today

Here's one thing that will bring immediate help: agree not to interfere with the parent who takes on the current parenting task. If your spouse begins the process when discipline and training are necessary, do not undermine and/or try to change what he/she is doing. Let them handle it without any interference. If you have an issue with the way they handled it, take it up with them gently and respectfully later, when you're alone and things have settled down.

CHAPTER 19

Zelophehad's Daughters:

Giving Your Children Value

Zelophehad son of Hepher had no sons; he had only daughters, whose names were Mahlah, Noah, Hoglah, Milcah and Tirzah. (Numbers 26:33)

*W*hat was Zelophehad thinking when he named his daughters? For that matter, what was Zelophehad's dad thinking when he named *him*? Tucked into the Book of Numbers is a really cool story about this family with the hard-to-pronounce names.

Zelophehad died during the forty-year wandering in the wilderness and never had any sons, but did have five daughters. So when it came time for Moses to count the people and tribes and decide who was going to get which land, his daughters wouldn't have received anything, because a father's inheritance got passed to his sons. No doubt many girls found themselves in this predicament, but we have no record of anyone else saying anything. Zelophehad's five, however, went to Moses to talk to him about what they considered an injustice (Numbers 27:1–11; 36:1–12; Joshua 17:3–6).

They pleaded their case and Moses talked to God about it. The Lord told Moses that the girls were right, and that if a man had no sons, his land should pass to his daughters. Not only did they get land, but because they spoke up about something that didn't seem right, their story made it into the Bible and the Israelites amended their inheritance law.

What did Zelophehad do to raise such self-confident daughters? To find out, let's jump back to exactly "what he was thinking" when he named his daughters.

It's important to remember that the Israelites didn't choose a name for their children simply because it sounded nice. They gave their children names that meant something and recalled a feeling, an event, or sometimes a calling. Also keep in mind that having sons was a big deal for the Israelites, and having daughters was considered a distant second best.

Zelophehad named his first daughter Mahlah, which means "sickness." The Hebrew word could denote travail or pain in childbirth. We don't know the details behind why she got her name, but one thing's for sure: he didn't focus on the wonder of his daughter.

He named his second daughter Noah, which is not the same as get-your-rain-gear Noah. This name means "movement." It could also mean to wander. Once again, Dad's thoughts seem turned toward his own circumstances. Perhaps he was growing tired of all of the wandering in the desert, with no son to be his pride and joy.

His third daughter got the name Hoglah, which means "a partridge." Looking at his little third-born, he must have decided that she looked like a cute, little bird. It took Zelophehad this long to get his eyes off of himself and onto the gifts God was giving him.

The name of the fourth-born, Milcah, means "queen." Now we're talking! This man, after fathering three girls and watching them grow and play and learn, began to realize how much these girls meant to him and how valuable they were.

So could the progression in the meanings of the names be coincidental? Not likely. Look at the name of the last daughter, Tirzah, which means, "delightsomeness." What are the odds of having five girls and no boys? In that culture, you might think that he would have felt hugely disappointed. But, no—instead, he felt great delight.

God gave Zelophehad five daughters and no sons and taught him something worth learning today. When you value your children highly, no matter what you may at first think of them, you will most likely end up with children who grow up to value themselves. They value themselves as God made them, not wishing they were someone else or were created differently.

When the five girls stood before Moses, they asked, *"Why should our father's name disappear from his clan because he had no son?"* They spoke well of their father and defended his name and his rights because they valued him. Children given value learn to value others.

It makes me chuckle that their question implies another question: "Are we less valuable than sons, and our father less valued because he didn't have sons?" Clearly they had been shown their value and felt that they and their father should be treated as people of value.

Their manner of speaking to Moses showed that they valued his position and authority, and they let Moses know that they weren't complaining or coming with a rebellious attitude; they merely wanted to bring before him a matter that they deemed worthy of his consideration. In the end, the girls got what they wanted.

Children who feel valued don't feel the need to fight and claw and rebel to get what they want.

Even if you already value your children, they won't know it and benefit from it unless you show it.

Here's a simple but powerful way to show your children that you value them: give them your undivided attention when they ask for it, listen intently when they speak, and never, ever brush them off or ignore them. Even if you're busy putting out fires or they're interrupting, you can stop and lovingly correct them and let them know when you'll be ready and happy to talk.

When your children blow it, make a mistake, or even disobey, be careful to maintain their value in the midst of correction. Don't call them names or put them down. Before you start correcting them, affirm their value by letting them know that you think the world of them and that we all make mistakes. Teaching, training, and correction is always better received from someone who you know values you.

Now we know what Zelophehad was thinking when he named his daughters and what he seems to have done right as a parent. Unfortunately, however, I looked up Zelophehad's

name and it comes from an unknown Hebrew root word—
so we still don't know what *his* dad was thinking.

Practical Parenting TIPS *For Today*

Tell your children any stories you have about their birth that describe how wonderful you felt when they arrived, how adorable you found them to be, and how incredibly blessed you felt (and still feel) to have them. Look for opportunities to affirm their value with your words. It's good to praise them for their accomplishments, but take care to value them beyond their performance; focus more on the worthy and special person your child is.

CHAPTER 20

Moses' Instructions to Israel's Parents:

Teaching from Life's Instruction Manual

*M*oses sat the Israelites down by the Jordan River and gave a *very* long sermon, relating the Law to them a second time and giving them God's instructions for how they should serve the Lord in the Promised Land. That sermon is the Book of Deuteronomy.

Many consider the sixth chapter of Deuteronomy to contain the heart of Moses' message. When Jesus talked about the greatest commandment, he referenced verses 5 and 6 from this chapter. Loving God and serving him wholeheartedly is the central theme of Moses' address.

Three times in this chapter, Moses reminds the Israelites that they must pass their faith on to their children so that future generations would continue to love God and walk in his blessings.

> *So that you, your children and their children after*
> *them may fear the LORD your God as long as you live by*
> *keeping all his decrees and commands that I give you,*
> *and so that you may enjoy long life.* (Deuteronomy 6:2)

That's the first reference. In the next two, Moses told the Israelites very practically how to accomplish the task. We'll look at one of them in this chapter and the second one in the next.

> *These commandments that I give you today are to be*
> *upon your hearts. Impress them on your children. Talk*
> *about them when you sit at home and when you walk*
> *along the road, when you lie down and when you get up.*
> *Tie them as symbols on your hands and bind them on*
> *your foreheads. Write them on the doorframes of your*
> *houses and on your gates.* (Deuteronomy 6:6–9)

My daughter and I made up a term for words that sound funny and are just plain fun to say. The word is *pid*. Everyone has different pids. I've always thought of the word *phylactery* as a pid. A phylactery is a little box containing Bible verses that religious Jews would literally strap onto their hands and foreheads in honor of these verses in Deuteronomy. The intent, however, was always to take God's Word to heart (v. 6) in every moment of the day and then to act on it. We are to teach our children that the Bible is life's handbook; we need to live our lives according to the Book.

So how do we show our children that the Bible gives us instruction in every area of life and help them learn what it is? Let's break down Moses' teaching.

When you sit at home: Teach and show your children that

God's Word and instruction should govern your family life. Teach them what it says and demonstrate how you live it. I'm sure most of us have told our children that the Bible instructs them to honor and obey us—but how about the rest of it: husbands loving their wives, wives respecting their husbands, husbands and wives treating each other well, forgiving one another and speaking kindly to one another, parents treating their children in love, not provoking them to anger or discouragement? Even if we struggle with some of these things, if we teach our children what God says about how a family operates and talk them through it as we do it or as we grow, they'll learn how to run their family by the Book.

When you walk along the road: How do you show your children to live God's way in your community? You do so when you walk in your neighborhood, buy groceries, attend church, and basically just go about your life? You do so as you hold your cool when another driver does something stupid and then talk about what the Bible says about patience. Let the children know that the Bible instructs you to do this; it's his plan for helping Christians to strengthen one another. When you discover that the clerk gave you too much change, return it and tell your children what the Bible says about honesty. If someone is in need, help them and talk about biblical love, mercy, and generosity.

When you lie down: By the end of the day or the weekend, it's time to rest. Choose your entertainment, showing your children that God's Word says we should guard our hearts.

When you get up: What thought first pops into our head when we get up? What does today hold, what does God have in store? When it's time to move or change jobs, or even make a tough choice, let your children hear that you're praying about it and trusting God to direct you. Look up your favorite verses on guidance, direction, and giving God control of your life, and show your children that you are living by the Book.

Tie them as symbols on your hands: Our hands represent all that we do. Whenever we do something out of a desire to honor God's Word, we should pause and tell our children what the Bible says that prompted our actions.

Bind them on your foreheads: This one's talking about phylacteries. Perhaps you could buy an arrangement of baseball caps with Bible verses printed on them. (I'm only joking.) This verse declares that the Bible should guide the way we think. Many Christians have gotten themselves in trouble because they thought God's Word is supposed to govern their actions only and not their thoughts—the old, "It's okay to think it as long as you don't act on it" line. Jesus called the Pharisees (the guys who wore phylacteries) "whitewashed graves" because they thought this way. Our thoughts and our hearts are interwoven, and our actions come out of our hearts. James said that sin comes from letting ourselves be drawn away and tempted by our own desires or thoughts (James 1:13–15). Fathers, when you're in public with your teenage son and a pretty girl goes by, talk to him about how to govern his thoughts. When someone sins against you or your children or does something to make one of you angry, don't talk only about what the Bible says; teach them what the Bible says about their thoughts and attitudes toward that person.

Write them on the doorframes of your houses. When Moses first spoke this command, the Israelites had no doorframes, only tent flaps. A few verses later, Moses warned them not to get so comfortable in the wonderful houses that God was going to provide that they forgot to serve God. Eventually Israel did forget God and got sucked into the habits of their pagan neighbors. When someone walks through your doorframe to visit, remember who gave you the house and your life, and don't change who you are. Teach your children to be sensitive and respect the rights of others to believe what they want, but not to change or hide who they are or to stop living according to God's Word just because someone else is around.

And on your gates: The Israelites lived in an agrarian society. For the most part, they lived in their house and worked on their property. This phrase represents living according to God's Word in the matter of choosing and functioning in our careers. When you make decisions at work, tough or otherwise, because of what you believe and what the Bible says, come home and tell your children the story.

Moses wanted to drive home the point that we need to teach our children that God's Word is lifes handbook. We need to teach them what it says and how to live it out. Learning Bible verses in Sunday school is wonderful, but unless we show our kids how to use them in life, where the rubber meets the road, they might as well just wear phylacteries (pid).

Practical Parenting TIPS  *For Today*

An easy, practical way to help your kids get into the habit of letting the Bible guide them in everything is to concretely demonstrate the process. First, choose an area where you need to remind yourself what God's Word says—if you tend to get impatient with other drivers, for example. Now find a verse that will help you battle inner road rage, such as Galatians 5:22–23, write part of it out on a sticky note, and stick it on your dashboard. Once you've explained this "reminder" system to your children, they'll be the first to point to it when you need to read it—but they'll also be watching you work through it. After they've watched you, help them choose an area and post a verse that correlates.

Point out to your children, however, that God said he'd write his Word on our hearts (Jeremiah 31:33) and that the Holy Spirit will remind us of those words (John 14:26) when we need them. In other words, once we've learned what God's Word says and have chosen to follow it, God works the process with active sticky notes on the inside of us that won't fall off or get forgotten. The sticky notes are just a way of showing them how to cooperate with God's system of changing us from the inside out.

CHAPTER 21

Moses on Testimonies:

Telling Your Children Faith Stories

In the future, when your son asks you, "What is the meaning of the stipulations, decrees and laws the LORD our God has commanded you?" tell him: "We were slaves of Pharaoh in Egypt, but the LORD brought us out of Egypt with a mighty hand. Before our eyes the LORD sent miraculous signs and wonders—great and terrible—upon Egypt and Pharaoh and his whole household. But he brought us out from there to bring us in and give us the land that he promised on oath to our forefathers."
(Deuteronomy 6:20–23)

What might be a good, modern application of Moses' advice to parents in Deuteronomy 6:20-23? Should we take out a Bible storybook and read the kids some Old Testament stories?

That would be a good start and we should familiarize our children with all of the wonderful stories in God's Word—but Moses really wants us to take his advice on a much more personal level.

In their younger years, my children loved it when I told them stories of all sorts. When we traveled to and fro in the car or at bedtime or during any opportune moment, one or more of my kids would ask for a story. They loved real stories from our family. They liked it when I'd ask them to name two animals and a weird gadget, and would make up a story using those elements. They also loved it when I'd tell them impromptu Bible stories. The stories that they requested most, though, were something that we called Faith Stories.

One day while driving with the kids, my mind was on another planet. When they realized I was mentally absent, they realized their need for a story. The requests varied, but in my fatigue, nothing of the usual story routine appealed to me. As my mind meandered back from its trip to outer space, a strange story from a long way back popped into the vacuum.

I told them about a time before they were even a thought. I was completely broke at the time and needed twenty dollars. In prayer I asked God for the money and felt sure that he had heard me and would provide. At the end of the day, I took out my wallet to get out a piece of ID—and there found a crisp twenty dollar bill. I knew my wallet had been empty at the beginning of the day, and it had remained in my pocket all day. Of course, I drew the story out, going over every detail. When I finished, the barrage of questions amazed me. Then they asked me to tell another story of answered prayer, and then another and another until we arrived at our destination.

Faith Stories became such a popular request that I spent several hours wracking my brains one afternoon and writing down a list of reminders of all the things I'd seen God do in my life. I wanted my Faith Story guns loaded and ready to go.

Moses didn't instruct the Israelites to tell ancient stories from someone else's experiences; he wanted the people to tell their children about what happened to them. Yes, he wanted the original stories to get passed on, but he also wanted later stories to get added. In my own experience, I discovered that stories of what God did in my life seemed to inspire the faith of my children in a way different than Bible stories did, perhaps because they seem more recent and more personal.

After I started telling Faith Stories, each one of my children's prayer lives and personal faiths took a leap forward. And before long my children were coming up to me and saying, "Dad, guess what! I've got a Faith Story."

Practical Parenting TIPS *For Today*

You, too, have Faith Stories. Write them down and have them ready to share with your children. If you have trouble remembering your own Faith Stories, take a few moments to think about a time God saved you from physical harm, met a need in a surprising way, healed a sickness, sent a friend, provided comfort through nature, answered a prayer. We all have many Faith Stories. In sharing them with your children, you will also refresh and encourage your own faith!

CHAPTER 22

Two Generations of Israelites:

Growing with Your Children

*I*magine yourself as a Hebrew child who left Egypt in the Exodus with your parents. Let's say you were eight at that time (probably born around 1454 B.C), old enough to have memories of Egypt, not only of everyday life, but also of slavery. You would have felt afraid when the Egyptian army came after you, but in awe as you watched the Red Sea open up so that you could walk through it.

Memories of growing up in the desert would abound since you wandered there until you were close to fifty. Some of those memories would include seeing your parents struggle with this guy, Moses, and his brother, Aaron.

You probably would have grown sick of manna, but you would have walked through years of seeing the older generation get it wrong and get hurt for it, and finally get it right and be rewarded for it. You would have miraculously crossed the Jordan, taken part in the triumph over Jericho, and settled your family in the long-awaited Promised Land.

Now try to imagine that you were born sixty years later, probably around 1394 B.C. You grew up in a nice home on a big, wonderful, and fruitful piece of property. Perhaps your dad went off from time to time, helping Joshua in his further conquests of the Promised Land; but otherwise, life was good. You may have heard about a journey that your parents or grandparents took through the wilderness, and about some guy named Moses, but he'd been dead for a dozen years before you were born. You were a teenager when, shortly before he died, Joshua gathered the leaders of Israel and got everyone to say that they "would serve the LORD," but you probably thought of that as just some religious thing. You hung out with some Canaanites and found out that everyone had different ideas about religion.

I've always found it strange that the generation of Israelites called stubborn and "stiff-necked," (Exodus 32:9) who were condemned to die in the wilderness, raised a generation of outstanding Israelites who served God and conquered Canaan. Conversely, the generation who conquered the Promised Land raised a generation who didn't know or follow God.

> *Joshua son of Nun, the servant of the LORD, died at the age of a hundred and ten. And they buried him in the land of his inheritance, at Timnath Heres in the hill country of Ephraim, north of Mount Gaash. After that whole generation had been gathered to their fathers, another generation grew up, who knew neither the LORD nor what he had done for Israel. Then the Israelites did evil in the eyes of the LORD and served the Baals.* (Judges 2:8–11)

Shouldn't it be almost a foregone conclusion that godly parents raise godly children, and that ungodly parents tend to raise ungodly children? Not necessarily so. As I dug deeper, two things in the story jumped out as keys to raising godly kids. That first generation had them, while the second one did not.

Moses warned the generation that crossed over the Jordan to make sure that they continued to serve God and to be sure that they told their children all of their faith stories. Unfortunately, it seems that the parents (or soon-to-be parents) were not listening or learning: "another generation grew up, who knew neither the LORD nor what he had done for Israel."

We've already discussed the second key, about letting our kids know what God has done for us. But I've found the first key very encouraging. The verse above says that the second generation didn't know the Lord. The word *know* doesn't mean "know about," but implies "to know personally," like you know a close friend. The children who grew up in the wilderness watched their parents struggle and blow it, learn, and eventually get it right. They watched and experienced firsthand spiritual growth, with all of its struggles and victories, and in that way learned how to get to know God.

The generation raised in the comfort of the Promised Land, however, for the most part had parents who felt content with their lives and who had ceased pushing forward with God.

Unfortunately, when we put God on the back burner and check in on him only on Sundays, we grow lethargic in our faith and start moving backward. We become more focused on our lives here and less focused on eternity. Children raised in this kind of atmosphere do not experience or learn how to get to know God. Even if they're getting a little doctrine at church, if they lack a home example of how to live the faith— if they grow up learning that being a Christian is merely believing the right things, instead of growing personally in Christ and with God—then probably they will wind up in sad spiritual shape.

The generation of parents who got it right messed up and struggled. Yet they kept seeking God, kept learning and growing, and thereby demonstrated how to get to know God. So the encouraging part of all of this is that we, like those parents struggling in the wilderness, don't have to be spiritual giants and get it all right in order to raise godly kids.

Being a Christian isn't about being perfect overnight or pretending to be perfect. It's about growing day-by-day in God's grace. I believe one of the most powerful ways to impact our children's lives for Christ is to let them know that we mess up and sin, but we're committed to the Lord and are growing right alongside them, walking in faith together, in God's grace, day after day.

Now imagine yourself as another child: one of your own. Ask yourself what they are learning and seeing from your example. If you feel stalled in your faith, stop, pray, and write down some spiritual goals, start moving, and then share your movement with your kids. If you're already moving, even if you're struggling, start looking for ways to grow spiritually with your children so that they can grow up knowing him. Then they, too, can conquer the "promised lands" that God has waiting for them.

Practical Parenting **TIPS** *For Today*

If we give our children the idea that we're perfect and don't let them see us struggle and grow, then they probably won't learn how to grow spiritually. You can have a long way to go with God, but if you're willing to seek him, apply yourself to spiritual growth, and remain transparent about it, then you're in a great position to raise godly children.

CHAPTER 23

Samson's Parents:

Explaining the Reasons Behind the Rules

The story of Samson, the powerhouse judge of Israel, offers a fascinating and captivating tale. When the Spirit of God came on him, he did awesome feats of physical strength. Once, when the Philistines tried to pen him in by closing the city gates, he got up in the night and tore away the gates, including the huge posts and crossbeam. If that weren't enough, he carried them to the top of a nearby hill and left them there.

Strangely though, he attacked the Philistines not because they sinned against Israel, but because he got mad at them for personal reasons. He killed a bunch of them and stole their clothes, because his Philistine wedding guests angered him for cheating at a riddle game he invented. He tied torches between the tails of 150 pairs of foxes and set them loose to burn down the Philistines' grain because his father-in-law gave Samson's promised wife to another man. Then, when the Philistines killed his betrothed and her family for bringing trouble on them, he went berserk and killed his enemies left, right, and center.

When the Philistines had the audacity to gather an army against him, he picked up the jawbone of a donkey and killed a thousand troops. At the end of his life, he pushed their temple down, killing thousands of them, along with himself. Why'd he do it? To get back at them for gouging out his eyes.

Samson, a man called by God, seems like a walking contradiction. Not only did he appear driven by revenge and anger, but he also slept with prostitutes—and in the end, seemed to treat even his Nazirite vow with contempt (see Numbers 6:2–5).

You probably know the story. Time and time again his female companion, Delilah, asked him to reveal the secret to his strength. He responded with a series of lies, which she quickly discovered when she tried to use the bogus information against him. She continued to nag him for the truth, and eventually he gave in and told her the secret of his strength: he'd become weak if someone cut off his hair. Surprise, surprise, she let in the barber while he slept, and his enemies easily captured him. After all the previous incidents, he must have known she would betray him; perhaps he had begun to imagine that his strength didn't really come from God but lay within himself. Either that, or he just didn't think.

I believe we can learn some valuable lessons from what the Bible tells us about Samson's parents. Not only will they help us to better comprehend Samson, but they can also teach us how to become better parents.

Manoah was Samson's dad. Manoah's wife got a visit from

an angel who told her about the son she would have, what he would do for Israel, and what she was to do with this special child. The angel barred her from eating anything unclean or to drink any alcohol during her pregnancy, and her son was to be a Nazirite—person set apart for God. No razor was to touch his head and he was never to drink alcohol.

Since Manoah missed the angel's visit, he prayed for him to come back.

> *Then Manoah prayed to the LORD, "O LORD, I beg you, let the man of God you sent to us come again to teach us how to bring up the boy who is to be born."*
> (Judges 13:8)

So when the angel appeared again, Manoah popped the question, but this time he got a little more specific about what he wanted to know.

> *So Manoah asked him, "When your words are fulfilled, what is to be the rule for the boy's life and work?"*
> (Judges 13:12)

The angel almost seemed to ignore his question, because he merely repeated what he had already told Manoah's wife, information Manoah already knew.

I find interesting what Manoah asked the angel. He asked about the "rule" for his son. The word *rule* in this form is "verdict," or "formal decree." The angel merely repeated what was said on his first visit because the only "divine decree" for this particular boy already had been given to Manoah's wife.

It appears that Manoah wanted a list of rules and regulations to give to his son, the divine decree for everything, the "thou shalts" and "thou shalt nots." But the Israelites already had the writings of Moses, which taught that children should be raised and taught to think through and apply God's Word to every aspect of their lives (Deuteronomy 6:7–9). They were to be taught God's Word and how to govern their thoughts, choices, and actions with it.

Apparently Manoah didn't get it, because it seems that Samson learned only how to follow the rules the angel gave his mother—and even that resolve fell apart in the end.

When Samson wanted to marry a Philistine, he demanded that his parents make the arrangements. When his parents suggested that he marry an Israelite, they didn't help him understand why such a course of action was better; they just made the suggestion and then caved in to Samson's demand. We have no record of Samson having an inner struggle with his actions; he just did whatever he wanted to do.

When we teach our children what God's Word says about how to live, we also need to give them the "why" whenever possible. Our children need the reason with the rule. I do not believe that the old parental fallback, "because I said so," or, "because God said so," is ever entirely appropriate.

When we teach our children to obey from the head (slavishly following a list of rules), instead of from the heart (understanding and delighting in the right choice), we don't teach them to think and choose for themselves. Consequently, when they don't have a concrete rule regarding an issue, they will often make bad choices; and when it suits them, they'll find ways around the rule. Why? Because the principle never becomes part of who they are and how they think; instead, it's just something tacked on from the outside. When we teach them why things are right and wrong, and then help them to understand, the principle becomes part of them. As a result, they become equipped to make the right choice, no matter what.

Consider lying, for example. The Bible doesn't just give the rule; it also supplies the reason. Once we look at what the Bible teaches about truth, we understand that truth is its own defense and that telling the truth garners people's trust, which strengthens relationships and opens opportunities. When we get in the habit of lying, we destroy trust and close off relationships. It's not enough just to tell children to avoid lying. We have to give them the rest of what the Bible teaches.

Sin isn't wrong merely because God doesn't like it; it's wrong because it's not how God created things to work, and doing it the wrong way messes up your life and the lives of other's. Help your children understand that God's unselfish love for us motivates his every instruction to us, and that what he instructs us to do is for our own good and makes sense.

The only commandment of the "big ten" aimed directly at children tells them to honor and obey their parents. But note that God didn't stop with the instructions and say, "because I said so." He added the reason: *"so that it may go well with you and that you may enjoy long life on the earth"* (Ephesians 6:3). In other words, if you listen to what your godly parents teach you and act on what you understand, things will go better for you. God wants us not only to give the rule, but also the reason and the reward.

I can't help but wonder how Samson might have changed the world if he had used his heart as powerfully as he used his physical strength. Even with all of his flaws, he wound up in the Bible's "Hall of Faith" (Hebrews 11:32). But what if his parents had taught him to love God with all of his heart and soul and strength and mind? Could he have become another Samuel? Or even another David?

We'll never know; his day is long past. Your own children's day, however, is just beginning. And the real question is this: what could *they* accomplish if you strive to do what Manoah never tried?

Practical Parenting
TIPS *For Today*

Take an extra minute to give your children the reasons behind the rules. This does not give children license to argue or compromise out of the rules. It helps them understand the concepts that led to the rules and the benefits they will receive from following the rules. Everyone, including children, is more likely to follow rules when they see direct benefits associated with following those rules.

CHAPTER 24

The Samuel Stages:

Spiritual Growth One Stage at a Time

*C*hild psychology has broken down childhood development into stages. Any one of a myriad of books can help you understand and cooperate with the psychological progress of your children.

I felt wonderfully delighted, yet not surprised, when, in my study of Samuel's childhood, I found that the Bible also recognizes childhood developmental stages. Samuel's story, however, focuses primarily on spiritual and/or faith growth, with a special emphasis on the stages a child goes through in developing a personal relationship with God.

The Bible gives report cards and/or updates regarding Samuel's growth at each stage of his childhood. By looking at these reports, we can gain insight into how our children should progress in their faith and relationship with God, and get an idea of what we can expect and how we can guide them through these stages.

Babies:

> *Hannah did not go. She said to her husband, "After the boy is weaned, I will take him and present him before the LORD, and he will live there always."*
> (1 Samuel 1:22)

It is our job as Christian parents to take charge of the discipleship of our children. Christian discipleship is a three-legged stool. Anyone who wants to grow as a Christian needs to grow in the knowledge of their faith; grow daily in their relationship with God; and grow personally, learning to apply what they've learned. The discipleship of children is no different; it simply happens at a different level.

Hannah had not been able to have children, so she made a deal with God that if he gave her a son, she would give the boy to God, to serve him all of his life. In response, God gave her Samuel. While the boy would grow up in and serve in the tabernacle, she recognized that she couldn't just take a baby and drop him off in a basket. So she stayed with her baby and loved him and nurtured him until he reached the age of about three.

Hannah teaches us that a child in this stage cannot be left to discover God on its own. It is imperative that we bring God to our children at this age and let them experience God's love and care while they experience ours.

The legs of the discipleship stool are greatly simplified at this stage, but all three should be present. A great way to ensure a daily, intentional focus on the discipleship of our children is to incorporate it into their bedtime routine: Bible stories, prayer, and discussion.

In this first stage, we can bring God to our children by reading them bedtime Bible stories and saying simple prayers.

Focus on God's love and simple truths and try your best to relate the prayers and the Bible story to your child's life. Prayers should be short and simple enough that they understand the point; and in discussing the story, do your best to associate something in it to something in their lives.

If at all possible, spend time doing this with each of your children individually. Help each child establish his or her own daily devotional time and personal relationship with God. If you gather the kid-pack together and try to do it *en masse*, that's a good thing, but you're teaching them about corporate worship, not individual devotions.

Preschool:

> *"So now I give him to the LORD. For his whole life he will be given over to the LORD." And he worshiped the Lord there.* (1 Samuel 1:28)

> *Then Elkanah went home to Ramah, but the boy ministered before the LORD under Eli the priest.* (1 Samuel 2:11)

After Samuel was weaned, Hannah made good on her promise and took him to the tabernacle to live and work. Little Samuel cooperates with the process, which signifies that Hannah had done a great job of teaching him who he was and how God had given him birth for a special purpose. He also starts to "minister before the LORD" right away, which shows that she taught him about God's plan for the Israelites and how to serve God.

While in the first stage the responsibility to introduce Samuel to God and the faith lay completely with Samuel's parents, in the next stage Samuel himself has responsibilities.

He is required to begin to serve God. Eli teaches and trains him, but Samuel must now do some of the work himself.

In this second stage, we need to be very proactive about beginning to transfer the focus from us doing it for a child to them responding on their own to God's truth. At bedtime, make your child aware that this is their time with God; start making a gradual transition from you saying their prayers to them praying with you. (And let them know when you spend your own time with God.)

When they're old enough to comfortably read out loud, begin to share that responsibility as well, with the goal of them doing it all for themselves when they feel ready. If they still like hearing a bedtime story, use another Christian book, perhaps just before their Bible and prayer time. Explain to them that as Christians we get to know God and are able to follow him when we spend time daily with him in prayer and Bible reading. Use this nighttime ritual to teach them how, but never lose sight of the goal: that they eventually do it on their own and continue throughout their life.

During this stage, put more emphasis on training your children to practice what they've learned in regard to Christian living, such as sharing a candy bar, getting along with their siblings, obedience, speaking, and responding politely. Training is essential at this stage. Try not to merely demand performance, but show them how to do it, give them suggestions, and gently reinforce the rule and the reason.

Elementary School Age:

> *But Samuel was ministering before the LORD—a boy wearing a linen ephod. Each year his mother made him a little robe and took it to him when she went up with her husband to offer the annual sacrifice.*
> (1 Samuel 2:18–19)

*And the LORD was gracious to Hannah; she conceived and gave birth to three sons and two daughters. Meanwhile, the boy Samuel **grew up** in the **presence of** the LORD.* (1 Samuel 2:21, emphasis added)

I like the way the author shows us rather than tells us that Samuel is growing and has moved into another stage. He paints a picture of Hannah returning annually with a new outfit. Your mind imagines the linen ephod getting larger each year.

"Samuel grew up in the presence of the LORD." In this stage, children don't just grow bigger; they begin the journey of "growing up." Part of growing up is that a child begins to think through and question what they're taught, checking for themselves if everything makes sense. Consequently, in this stage they need to become progressively more aware of the reality of God and their Christian faith. Samuel experienced this by growing "in the presence of the LORD."

Telling Faith Stories is a great way to help children see God in action and affirms the reality of what they believe. Questions they may have about how we know the Bible is God's Word and how, or if, evolution contradicts their faith, or even where dinosaurs fit, should be welcomed and addressed. Many wonderful books address those questions, along with many other questions your children may have. If you don't know the answers, just say so, and suggest that you find the answer together with your child—but don't put it off. Treat these queries with priority.

In this stage, their evening (or some other time, if it works better for your family) time with God is their own. Sit with them to help, teach, encourage, and make sure they're consistent; but by the end of this stage, they should be doing it on their own. Encourage them to avoid falling into the habit of praying the same way and reading from the same book every night. Their prayers should reflect their concerns, what they and those around them are going through, and what they need help with. If they need privacy, let them pray silently while you pray along. It's actually a good sign that they want to talk to God about stuff they'd rather not let others hear. Also their Bible-reading choices, when possible, should reflect what's happening in their lives, what questions they're asking, and/or even what sparks their curiosity.

Help them think through the consequences of their choices and actions. Point out real-life examples that demonstrate that, more often than not, wrong choices yield wrong results and good choices lead to positive results.

Preteen:

And the boy Samuel continued to grow in stature and in favor with the LORD and with men. (1 Samuel 2:26)

Luke patterned his description of Jesus' childhood after this report (Luke 2:40, 52). At this stage, children start to grow noticeably in stature (physically), and start to head toward, if not into, puberty. After alerting us to Samuel's physical stage, the author adds "in favor with the Lord and men" to his report.

Young children tend to be seen as an extension of their parents. Until they begin to really display their individuality, they are not readily acknowledged as "individuals" in their own right. In this stage, children start to emerge as who they really are. *They* grow in favor with God and men; in other words, they are increasingly seen and recognized for who they are and what they do as individuals, apart from their parents.

This is the bridge to self-awareness and self-assertiveness, the time when children decide what they believe and who they are going to be. This stage is therefore crucial to the faith development of your child.

In their nightly times with God, encourage them to take the initiative. Lead them to start using a full-text Bible, as opposed to a Bible storybook. If it's time for a new Bible, take them to the bookstore and let them pick out one they'd like. If they're ready to start meeting with God alone, take care not to let it drop off your radar screen. Go into their room and talk with them, and be sure that they're set up and ready to go. Talk to them a little more like a peer; tell them what you're currently reading and praying about in your quiet times. Often the transition between time with Mom or Dad reading Bible stories, and time alone reading the Bible, is not guided and guarded, and the bridge stage does not get properly crossed. Give them room to grow, but not enough room to fall off the bridge.

In this stage, church involvement should become more individualized. Help your children get more involved at church and find friends and other reasons why they like to be there. When your child reaches the right age, do everything that you can do to plug them into a growing church youth group. Also, do everything in your power to help your child make the correct friendship choices.

Teenager:

> The LORD came and stood there, calling as at the other times, "Samuel! Samuel!" Then Samuel said, "Speak, for your servant is listening." (1 Samuel 3:10)

> *The LORD was with Samuel as he grew up, and he let none of his words fall to the ground. And all Israel from Dan to Beersheba recognized that Samuel was attested as a prophet of the LORD. The LORD continued to appear at Shiloh, and there he revealed himself to Samuel through his word. And Samuel's word came to all Israel.*

(1 Samuel 3:19–4:1)

Ah, the teenage years. Did you notice that the above report does not say that Samuel rebelled for a while, thought that adults were out of touch, and that he fell away from his faith?

This final, glorious stage begins with the story of God speaking to the young Samuel and trusting him with important information. By this time, our child's prayers should be getting more intimate and personal, and they should concern their struggles and not just their desires. They should definitely conduct their time with God on their own; but still check in and encourage them to be consistent, just like you would check that they're eating properly.

Also, continue to openly discuss with them their faith walk by describing what you're learning, reading, praying about, or struggling with.

Luke gave two reports about Jesus' growth that borrowed heavily from the Samuel narrative. Since Luke did a thorough job of investigative reporting and talked to many witnesses about everything he wrote down, he probably got some details of Jesus' birth and childhood from Mary herself, or from some other knowledgeable family member. The fact that Luke borrows from the Samuel reports, and that Mary knew Hannah's song and story, suggests that the Samuel stages might have provided some helpful guidelines to Mary and Joseph.

When Joseph and Mary had done everything required by the Law of the Lord, they returned to Galilee to their own town of Nazareth. And the child grew and became strong; he was filled with wisdom, and the grace of God was upon him. (Luke 2:39–40)

And Jesus grew in wisdom and stature, and in favor with God and men. (Luke 2:52)

Life has many stages, and Christian growth is meant to be daily and progressive—for children as well as for adults. It was for Samuel and it was for Jesus. Our goal is to teach, train, and prepare our children for life on their own and to get them ready to start growing in and through adulthood. Our goal for their spiritual lives is no different. By the time they become ready to build their own nests, we want to help them develop a mature relationship with God, a solid understanding of their faith, and to find a healthy place in a Christian community.

We help them get there by encouraging them to move one step and one day at a time—not expecting growth to happen by osmosis and also not pushing them beyond their stage in life. God's plan is wonderful—it allows children time to grow into their own faith as it allows parents time to grow in wisdom.

Practical Parenting TIPS  *For Today*

Consider a few suggestions for developing a fruitful devotional time appropriate for a child at varying developmental stages:

Baby: Introduce your baby to the concepts of God's love, God's creation, and God's care.

Preschool: Help your child understand that it's important to have a quiet time with God. At first do this with the child, and then slowly begin to transfer the responsibility. Read Bible stories together and teach the child how to pray.

Elementary: Have your children read the Bible themselves, ask questions of you to assure a proper understanding, and provide whatever guidance they might need to form their own devotional thoughts.

Preteen: By this stage, the child should begin having an independent devotional time, alongside the parent. Have the child pray both independently and together with you.

Teen: Teens should be enjoying their own devotional time with the Lord. Let teens see you having your own devotional time. Talk with them about interesting things you have discovered in your own devotional time. Pray daily for your child.

CHAPTER 25

Samual at the Temple:

It Takes a Parent— Don't Dump It All on the Village

$\mathcal{S}$amuel didn't grow up taking regular trips to the tabernacle; instead, the "numero uno" spiritual guy in Israel raised him in the tabernacle. And so he grew up to become one of God's great heroes.

So then, maybe we've finally hit on the real key to raising godly kids: it's obviously the church's responsibility, right?

Well, maybe not.

Eli's sons, who also either grew up at the tabernacle or attended there regularly with their dad, ended up stealing from their own people, sleeping with the women who served at the tabernacle, and became such evil men that God finally killed them in judgment.

Okay, so maybe these two guys were just bad apples? Or perhaps Eli just wasn't very good at the whole dad thing? Unfortunately for the "let the church do it" theory, another bit of information really throws the proverbial monkey wrench into the whole idea.

The very first time God spoke to Samuel, he revealed his intent to judge Eli's whole family because *"his sons made themselves contemptible, and he failed to restrain them"* (1 Samuel 3:13).

Samuel grew up watching the evil antics of Eli's sons, as well as Eli's lack of restraint. So when it came time for him to take Eli's place and also raise two sons of his own in or around the tabernacle, you'd think he'd get it right. Right?

Wrong!

> *When Samuel grew old, he appointed his sons as judges for Israel. The name of his firstborn was Joel and the name of his second was Abijah, and they served at Beersheba. But his sons did not walk in his ways. They turned aside after dishonest gain and accepted bribes and perverted justice.* (1 Samuel 8:13)

What is the problem? For a minute it looked as if dropping the kids off at church was the solution. Could it be that what Samuel saw *modeled* in Eli's family impacted him even more than what he was taught? That Eli's actions spoke louder than his words?

The Lord, through Moses, gave the Israelites specific instructions about how to raise their children. The parents were to actively seek God and live God's way as an example, and share their stories and lives of faith with their children. Also, they were to teach their children God's Word, help them to understand it, and train them how to apply it to every aspect of their lives. Of course, going to and serving God at the tabernacle was part of the training, because these visits were a big part of what God required.

Sadly, the Israelites did not serve God and did not follow God's plan for teaching and training their children. Samuel grew up under better circumstances because his mother made a special effort to do it right while she weaned her son, and then, perhaps, the older-but-wiser Eli made a better mentor to Samuel than he had been a father to his own boys. But Samuel still saw the actions modeled in the home between Eli and his sons, and apparently they skewed his parental understanding.

Either way, Samuel's good upbringing was an anomaly, a sovereign exception; and since we tend to raise children based on the knowledge and experience that we gain from our parents, Samuel was ill equipped to raise his boys God's way. Being a godly person does not make you a good parent, anymore than being a good accountant means that all of your children will handle money wisely. Parenting God's way takes learning, effort, practice, and intentionality. Still, it's a whole lot easier if you've been parented God's way, because when you fall back on your experience, you're automatically moving in the right direction.

We in the body of Christ, like the Israelites of Samuel's day, have a great challenge before us. According to a Gallup poll, only 30 percent of children raised in the church decide to stay there by the time they're eighteen. In other words, we are losing *70 percent* of our children, at least for a time, to the world. And we're losing them for the same two reasons that plagued Samuel's generation:

1. We're not following God's biblical model for raising our children with a personal, fully integrated faith.

2. Somewhere along the way, we bought into the idea that we should let the "professionals" raise our children.

We send them to school and don't give a whole lot of thought to what they're being taught because "that's the teacher's job." As the generations have gone by, this ideology has gobbled up more and more parental territory, like the spread of gangrene.

Eventually the professionals started to feel that they could do a better job of training our children in regards to life issues, as well. So they took over sex education. Then when our kids started getting a little heavy, the school took on the teaching of diet, exercise, and nutrition. And a funny thing began to take place in our society: the more the professionals took on, the more the parents of each passing generation got the idea that it was up to the professionals to teach their children more and more of what used to be the parents' job. So they let go of even more.

Then government studies showed that our children were graduating from high school with next to no life skills. So the professionals, with all good intentions, raced to put courses in our schools that taught children everything, from how to do their banking to how to select a career.

The whole process has taken many years because the gangrene spreads only a little further with each generation; but we've now arrived at a place where the primary task for all parents is to house, feed, clothe, and entertain their children, while all teaching and training is someone else's concern.

And how does this cultural gangrene fit into faith training? To whom do most Christian parents look to provide the spiritual training of their children? The church. Certainly churches have given a yeoman's effort to make up for a lack of parental faith training. The church has responded with more and bigger programs for children, working to the point of exhaustion to spiritually train the children placed in their care.

But it's not working—and it's not working because it's not the way God told us to do it. God's plan for teaching children has not changed since he set it up with Abraham and taught it to the Israelites through Moses. Hear what Paul has to say:

> *Fathers, do not exasperate your children; instead,* **bring them up in the training and instruction of the Lord.** (Ephesians 6:4, emphasis added)

Paul does not advise us to add Christian doctrine or teaching and prayers and Bible stories to the overall mix of our children's lives. He said, "Bring them up in the training and instruction of the Lord." He's saying essentially the same thing Moses did: make God's Word the foundation for everything you teach your children, and train them to live according to its wisdom.

Did you notice something else? Neither Moses nor Paul mentioned the tabernacle and the priest, nor the church and the children's pastor. Why not?

It's the parents' job.

Why do parents have the responsibility of training their children in godliness? Remember the three legs of Christian discipleship: growing in the knowledge of your faith; growing daily in your relationship with God and growing personally; and learning to apply what you've learned to who you are and what you do. The church can be a great aid in helping a child grow in the knowledge of the faith, but it cannot supply the other two legs.

In order to bring children into a closer daily walk with God, *you* have to train them daily, because you're with them every day. Also, in order to teach and train children to apply what they've learned, you have to be there when the fight erupts, when the last cookie gets selfishly grabbed, and when the fit is thrown. God knows what he's doing, and the Bible never tells us that we should leave the spiritual training of children to anyone else, because parents are the *only* ones in a position to practically and successfully get the job done.

Children look to your example more closely than to any other. Eli probably never imagined how much his teaching and training and family interaction with his own sons would affect Samuel and future generations.

Samuel's generation did not serve or follow God, and therefore their children did not get properly trained. Each generation grew progressively worse as parents slid further and further away from God's program. Samuel's childhood provided a bright spark in a cavern of deep darkness, but it could not be readily replicated because it was a sovereign exception. *It never was, and still isn't, God's plan for us to completely rely on the church for all of the spiritual training of our children.*

If you read Samuel's story closely, you won't find God telling Hannah to take Samuel to the tabernacle; the Scripture attributes the idea to Hannah (1 Samuel 1:11, 22). Now, don't get me wrong. God knows the beginning from the end and he worked everything out in Samuel's life, according to his purposes. Since all of Scripture screams again and again, however, that the spiritual training of children is the task of parents, we must see this episode as a divine exception. The fact that Samuel could not replicate his experience, but instead ended up with results similar to what happened to Eli's sons, adds more compelling evidence of this as an exception.

The bulk of credit for Samuel's godly upbringing must be given to Hannah for what she did in the formative years before her son moved to the tabernacle. Church programs are great; they help us in our task. Nevertheless, we have to take back our God-given responsibility to teach and train our children daily to walk with God and to live according to the handbook for life that he gave us. We must teach them about sex, finance, relationships, family, career choices, and every other area of their lives, in accordance to what God's Word says.

God does not limit his definition of *parent* to "provider and entertainer", the first line in God's definition reads, "teacher, trainer, and mentor."

Practical Parenting TIPS  *For Today*

The church cannot train your child for you, but it can hugely aid you in the process. Take your children to church and help them apply themselves to learning about God while they are there. Set up a meeting with whoever leads the children's program in your church and find out what's being taught. See if you can reinforce that teaching at home by finding a book that will help you teach the same thing at home. As your children get older, encourage them to get involved in the church's youth group. Also, see if your church has any classes or support for helping parents raise their children God's way—and be ready to help and volunteer. After all, you're the one with this book in your hands.

CHAPTER 26

Eli's Bad Boys:

The Difference Between Rebuke and Restraint

$\mathcal{E}$li's sons were bad eggs. These rebellious priests stole from, threatened, and even raped the people who came to Shiloh to meet God.

When God told young Samuel what he was going to do about the situation, he put his finger on the parenting problem that led to the demise of Eli's sons.

> *For I told him that I would judge his family forever because of the sin he knew about; his sons made themselves contemptible, and he failed to restrain them.*
> (1 Samuel 3:13)

If you read this story casually, God's words may seem confusing, especially because in the previous chapter we learn that Eli confronted and rebuked his sons for their behavior. And the narrative adds that his sons didn't listen because God had determined to put them to death (1 Samuel 2:22–26).

Why did God get on Eli's case if Eli had correctly rebuked his sons? And how could God blame Eli if his sons didn't listen because God caused them not to?

I believe we find the answers in the definition of two little words. To "rebuke" is to harshly criticize someone for something they've done; to "restrain" someone is to prevent them from doing it. Eli rebuked his sons, when God said he should have restrained them. This story demonstrates two ways to correct your children, one the wrong way and the other the right way. Let's look at the wrong way first.

Think of the classic picture of parents trying unsuccessfully to make their children behave in a public place. "Johnny, stop doing that. You know that you're not allowed to do that!" After the second or third round of failed attempts, out comes the question: "Why do you always do this when I take you out?" And then the threat: "Fine, I won't take you out anymore." Of course, none of these attempts works, so the parents attempt to take their children prisoners and/or remove them from the building . . . and then the screaming starts.

Eli's rebuke of his sons included the question, *"Why do you do such things?"* and reminded them of God's threats for disobedience.

I once visited a family that had a terror for a young daughter. She listened like a brick, disobeyed every request, and screamed and yelled and threw a fit whenever anyone tried to make her do anything. They asked if I could help. So after dinner, when the usual bedtime war erupted and she got dragged to her room, I asked if I could take over. The little girl was sitting defiantly on her bed when I entered the room. I sat down and started to gently talk with her. The more I talked, the more baffled she looked. Finally, she spoke: "Aren't you going to spank me?"

After recovering from the unexpected question, I asked why she thought I was going to spank her. "Because that's what you're supposed to do," she answered. "I do the wrong thing and yell and then I get sent to my room and get a spanking." This little girl's parents had introduced her to a dance and she had memorized the steps. In her mind, that's how life worked. She didn't think she was supposed to obey and cooperate; she believed that she was supposed to act up, get sent to her room, and be spanked.

We need to teach our young children the right dance steps—and we use restraint to do that. When your child does something wrong, remember that they need training. Don't just bark a command from across the room. When you bark, you are in no position to train or restrain. Go to your child and explain the rule and the reason, and help them to understand why it's important.

Next, walk them through the steps of how to do it correctly. Let's say that you called them for dinner and they purposely ignored you. Don't call a second time—go to where they are and explain how a family works better when everyone cooperates: someone makes the dinner, someone cleans up, and everyone comes when they're called so that all can enjoy a warm meal. Ask them if they understand, and after receiving an affirmative answer, let them know that you'd like to try it again. Don't go to the kitchen, however; stand right there, hold their hand, and ask them in your nicest voice to please go to the dinner table. Now start walking hand-in-hand toward the kitchen; then praise them when they get there.

Whatever you do, don't let them disobey or you'll create a dance that you won't want to live with. Suppose that when Mom calls me a few times for dinner, I sit and watch TV for a while longer; Mom screams at me to come for dinner, yet I watch more TV; and Dad finally grabs me and carries me to the table. If you create that dance and don't correct it, your children will perform it flawlessly every time, no matter how often you scream, protest, threaten, and ask *the* question.

By the way, physical restraint, as a last resort, is just another step in the dance when hands-on, gentle training doesn't precede it. To restrain your child is to show them how to obey, and then to lovingly and consistently make sure that they comply. If you consistently restrain your child from doing it wrong and walk them through doing it right, then you won't have to continually rebuke them and ask them why they always behave so terribly. When God delivered his message through Samuel, he answered the question that Eli asked his sons: *"Why do you do such things?"* They did so because he *"failed to restrain them."*

Restraint parenting takes more effort, but the rewards are huge—especially when you're an old priest, in the doctor's waiting room, or when you have some guy who writes parenting books over for dinner.

Practical Parenting
TIPS *For Today*

Have you allowed your children to set patterns of disobedience, even in small things? Whether it is a call to dinner or cleaning their room, children learn how far they can push and what steps will take place before parents deal with the issue. Select one area where they've fallen into a pattern of disobedience. Then, help your children understand the expectations and the consequences, walk them through the steps necessary to change that pattern. Patterns of obedience are just as easy to set as negative ones—but they bring harmony to the home and teach children self-control.

CHAPTER 27

Samuel and Eli:

Helping Your Child Get to Know God

Again the LORD called, "Samuel!" And Samuel got up and went to Eli and said, "Here I am; you called me." "My son," Eli said, "I did not call; go back and lie down." Now Samuel did not yet know the LORD. The word of the LORD had not yet been revealed to him. The LORD called Samuel a third time, and Samuel got up and went to Eli and said, "Here I am; you called me." Then Eli realized that the LORD was calling the boy. So Eli told Samuel, "Go and lie down, and if he calls you, say, 'Speak, LORD, for your servant is listening.' So Samuel went and lay down in his place. The LORD came and stood there, calling as at the other times, "Samuel! Samuel!" Then Samuel said, "Speak, for your servant is listening." (1 Samuel 3:6–10)

Samuel was around twelve years old when this wonderful event took place. I say "wonderful" because getting to know God and growing closer to him is the greatest blessing there is, in this life or the next. By looking at Samuel's story, we can glean some ideas that will help us lead our children into this wonderful blessing.

Samuel's mother taught him about God until he was weaned. When the time came to live at the tabernacle in Shiloh, he went willingly to fulfill her vow and immediately began helping Eli in God's service. Samuel served God in the tabernacle, was educated there, learned God's Word, and daily discovered how to apply what he knew of God and his Word to his character and actions so that he grew in favor with God and men. Yet this part of the story says, *"Samuel did not yet know the LORD: The word of the LORD had not yet been revealed to him."*

The biblical idea of "knowing God" goes beyond merely knowing facts *about* God. God wants us to know him in an intimate and personal way, in our hearts and in our experiences.

Eventually, of course, Samuel became a prophet. So is it fair to draw a parallel for raising Christian children today? I believe so, for the following reasons: In the Old Testament, the ministry of the Holy Spirit came primarily through God's chosen leaders, such as kings, priests, and prophets. The Holy Spirit revealed himself to these leaders in a very personal and experiential way. As Christians, we *all* have the Holy Spirit, who has been given the task of revealing God to us.

> *You, however, are controlled not by the sinful nature but by the Spirit, if the Spirit of God lives in you. And if anyone does not have the Spirit of Christ, he does not belong to Christ.* (Romans 8:9)

"And I will ask the Father, and he will give you another Counselor to be with you forever—the Spirit of truth. The world cannot accept him, because it neither sees him nor knows him. But you know him, for he lives with you and will be in you." (John 14:16–17)

"But when he, the Spirit of truth, comes, he will guide you into all truth. He will not speak on his own; he will speak only what he hears, and he will tell you what is yet to come." (John 16:13)

On the day of Pentecost when the disciples gathered according to Jesus' parting instructions, God poured out the Holy Spirit on the church. Peter explained that this amazing event fulfilled prophecy:

"In the last days, God says, I will pour out my Spirit on all people. Your sons and daughters will prophesy, your young men will see visions, your old men will dream dreams." (Acts 2:17)

The Israelites understood that, in their day, only special leaders participated in the ministry of the Holy Spirit; yet Joel declared that the Holy Spirit would be poured out on *everybody*. In order to make his point—that God would no longer reserve this blessing for the special one—she predicted that even the children would prophesy. *Everyone*, including kids, would experience God through the ministry of the Holy Spirit.

So how do we help our children experience God through the wonderful gift of the Holy Spirit? Let's take a look at Samuel's experience.

To start with, Samuel learned about God. Our children will find it hard to get to know God experientially if they don't know what he's like. Our understanding of God and what he's like will shape our ideas, our behavior, and our lives.

Explain to your children that part of getting to know God is learning all you can about him from his Word. It's just like when you're developing a friendship: you talk to them and find out who they are and what they are like. Look up Bible verses that help them understand that God is faithful, trustworthy, loving, kind, merciful, forgiving, just, all-powerful, all-knowing, everywhere all of the time, etc. We see God's character most fully and clearly revealed in the life of Jesus. Think of Jesus as God's show-and-tell (see Hebrews 1:3).

Next we see that Samuel had some coaching. God called Samuel three times, and each time Samuel mistook him for Eli. The old priest finally let Samuel know what was going on. Samuel had someone who could tell him that God wanted to speak to him and what to do about it.

Sometimes we can go through life and not know that God is trying to draw us closer and help us to know him better because no one has shown us how. Tell your children that God is not far away or trying to hide from them; he's very real and always with them, and he wants them to experience his love for themselves. Tell them stories of how you've experienced God in your own walk with him; times you've asked for wisdom and then had the solution enter peacefully into your thoughts; times you've felt convicted to do (or not do) something and what happened; times you've seen God in answered prayer; times when you've felt his presence in peace or comfort; times you've sought direction and sensed an answer, and then seen God confirm it through circumstances; times when you've struggled to understand and then had the Word of God come alive to you and bring the answer; and many other stories in which God has made himself very real to you. Each time God shows himself to us, even in the smallest way, he helps us better know him and what he's like.

Once my son asked me why he couldn't see God. He felt that God must be hiding from us. I prayed silently that God would give me wisdom. The answer popped into my heart and I explained that God doesn't want to hide from us at all. Our physical eyes were made to see physical things, not spiritual things. God is invisible, not because he's hiding, but because our physical eyes can't see him. We see or experience God in different ways. I asked my son to close his eyes, and I remained silent for a minute. Then I asked him if he knew I was still there, even with his eyes closed. I explained that when I close my eyes and spend time with God, he's very real and very present to me, because I've gotten to know him and have spent a lot of time with him. This really helped my son to start focusing his prayer on talking to a real God whom he was getting to know.

This episode led me to teach him how crucial it is for us to seek God. If we feel content to fire our prayer list at God and get on with living our lives, God will oblige us and give us all the room we need. When we seek him, however, asking him to help us to get to know him and experience him, he starts to draw closer to us and reveal himself in deeper ways. Teach your children to pray what I call "seek prayers" every night, asking God to draw them near. When Samuel learned that God was trying to talk to him, he went back to his bed and waited; his response showed that he wanted to hear from God.

Eli taught Samuel to respond to God by saying, *"Speak, LORD, for your servant is listening."* Teach your children to not hurry through their prayers, rattling off the usual list like they quote lines from favorite movies. Rather, wait. Listen. Prayer should be current and conversational. If they tend toward rote prayers, ask how they'd feel if, every time you spoke to them, you said the very same thing. In a conversation with God, you need to slow down and *think*.

Also, every conversation is two-sided. How is God going to make himself real to you, helping you sense his presence or putting wisdom in your heart about something you've prayed about, if you never stop talking and sit still? Teach your children to pause between prayers and to quietly reflect after they're finished, leaving time for God to settle their heart, give them peace, or drop another topic of prayer in their hearts.

Create in your children an expectation of experiencing God and, as Eli did for Samuel, help them recognize the signs of his presence.

Getting to know God is a lifelong pursuit, so don't feel that you have to suddenly make it happen. Pray about it, ask for wisdom and help, and then start looking for one-step-at-a-time opportunities to teach your children and encourage them in the wonderful and progressive journey called knowing God.

Practical Parenting  TIPS *For Today*

Here's a few suggestions for helping your children get to know God:

1. Teach them about God—who he is and what he's like.

2. Help them understand that God wants them to grow closer to him and experience him. He's not hiding.

3. Help them to really talk to God from their hearts, with their own words.

4. Encourage them to slow down and be quiet between the different things they pray about.

5. Talk to them about ways God has made himself real to you.

6. Teach them to seek God by asking him to help them get to know him better every day and to experience him.

7. Help them to recognize God by pointing out answered prayer and every way you see God working in their lives.

CHAPTER 28

David and Sons:

Don't Bury Your Issues and Feelings—Talk Them Out

David had at least eight wives, ten concubines, and ten sons. Four of his sons were born to Bathsheba, but every other son came from a different mother. By today's standards, this was a blended family on steroids—and David had a lot of trouble managing it.

I found it interesting that even though the Bible overflows with information on David and his family, I could find only one biblical comment regarding David's parenting habits. The Scripture records a fair amount of interaction between David and his children and describes many things that his children did. These verses don't draw conclusions about David's efforts, however. For the most part, they don't even refer to David as a "father," but instead refer to him as king or just David.

At the end of his life, just before he appoints Solomon as his successor, the Bible speaks for the first time of David's track record as a father.

> *Now Adonijah, whose mother was Haggith, put himself forward and said, "I will be king." So he got chariots and horses ready, with fifty men to run ahead of him. (His father had never interfered with him by asking, "Why do you behave as you do?" He was also very handsome and was born next after Absalom).*
>
> (1 Kings 1:5–6 emphases added)

First, note *the* notorious question that Eli had asked his sons: *"Why do you behave as you do?"* David didn't even go as far as Eli did; he never even asked the question! In all of the biblical record, you won't find him asking *the* question at all, or restraining his children, even though they committed some pretty serious infractions.

So what can we learn from the biblical record on David's parenting, and what does it mean that he "never interfered"?

At first we might think that David's royal duties forced him to become an absentee dad. He had a lot of Philistines and Amorites and various Canaanites to beat up, insurrections to handle, political infighting, and a difficult kingdom to rule. The Bible doesn't allow such a conclusion, however. David made himself available to his kids; they ate with him at the kings table and he even appointed his sons as royal advisors. So at work and at rest, David spent time with his children (2 Samuel 8:15–18; 9:11).

So . . . maybe he was there, but he didn't care? Again, not true. David loved his children deeply. He even penned this verse in the Psalms: *"As a father has compassion on his children, so the LORD has compassion on those who fear him"* (Psalm 103:13).

Well then, perhaps David didn't spend the time to teach his children, and/or he didn't care how they behaved? Unlikely. David was a godly man and knew from instruction and experience that pleasing God has a lot to do with one's behavior. The Bible tells us that it disturbed David greatly when his children misbehaved. We don't know if he spent as much time with his other kids as he did with Solomon, but Solomon tells us that his father taught him a great deal (Proverbs 4:3–9). David's royal family also had special tutors, and quite possibly received instruction from advisors and priests who formed part of David's court (1 Chronicles 27:32).

David's children received godly instruction, he spent time with them, he loved them deeply, and he cared how they behaved. So what was the problem? It seems that David had trouble speaking his mind to his children and talking through difficult issues with them, a possibility reflected in the one comment we have about David's parenting: *"His father had never interfered."*

When David's son, Amnon, raped his half-sister, Tamar, and then refused to marry her, the Bible records the fury of David—but it says nothing of what he might have said to the children involved. The incident infuriated Absalom, another of David's brood, and he took his sister in and cared for her; but it seems that—like father, like son—he also suffered from sweep-it-under-the-rug syndrome.

> *Absalom never said a word to Amnon, either good or*
> *bad; he hated Amnon because he had disgraced his sister*
> *Tamar.* (2 Samuel 13:22, emphasis added)

So the whole mess brewed as everyone stewed their bad feelings—until two years later, when Absalom killed his brother for raping Tamar. Again, David felt grieved and upset, but we have no record of him talking things through with Absalom. Absalom runs away to Geshur and lives with his grandfather, the king of Geshur, for three years. At any time David could have asked his father-in-law to send the kid home for a chat, or he could have made a short trip himself—but he never did. The Bible tells us that after three years, David finished grieving for Amnon and he *"longed to go to Absalom,"* but he still didn't visit him or send for him (2 Samuel 13:38–39).

When cooler heads finally convinced David to call Absalom back from Geshur, he did so, but refused to see his son. Finally, Absalom squirmed his way in to see David, and David kissed him—but that's all. Absalom was back on his dad's good side, but we see no mention of them talking through what had separated them.

The very next chapter describes Absalom's bloody attempt to take the throne from his father. For four years, Absalom plotted and openly worked his charm on the people, but still his dad said nothing to him.

Fast-forward many years to just before David's death, as another of his son's plots for the throne, trying to snatch it before it gets passed to his brother Solomon.

> *Now Adonijah, whose mother was Haggith, put*
> *himself forward and said, "I will be king." So he got*
> *chariots and horses ready, with fifty men to run ahead of*

him. (His father had never interfered with him by asking, "Why do you behave as you do?" He was also very handsome and was born next after Absalom).
(1 Kings 1:5–6)

Although David loved his children deeply and tried to be a good father, he failed to develop and use a very important parenting tool: the heart-to-heart talk.

Discipline and training comes easier with young children. It doesn't involve a ton of explaining and helping them to wrestle with issues and make right decisions. As they get older, however, the process gets more complicated. Your child develops a personality and a will, and often discipline must involve discussion, teaching, and reasoning things out. Because this isn't always easy, therefore conflict and resolving conflict becomes part of the discipline process.

If you tend to retreat from conflict, then it can feel easier to ignore or put off sitting your child down and working through what you know needs to be addressed.

Believe it or not, the Bible suggests that David, the giant killer, consistently shied away from personal conflict. When he blew it with Bathsheba, he tried to get her husband, Uriah, to sleep with her to cover his crime. When her husband refused, David could have confessed his sin and talked it out, but instead he had Uriah cleverly killed. His army commander, Joab, again and again did things his own way, and even killed in cold blood the men David had named as his successors—but David just let it slide. The examples multiply, especially when it came to his children.

When we know that our children are heading in the wrong direction, we need to take the time to take them aside and talk it through, no matter how difficult it may feel. When we tell ourselves, "they probably won't listen," or "they'll figure it out for themselves; I don't want to interfere," or "I'll deal with it some other time," we fool ourselves. We use those excuses to get us out of what we know we need to do.

I'm a people person. I don't like conflict and I like my children to like me; therefore, like David, I have often needed to deal with this issue. I've run the excuses through my head and caught myself putting off till tomorrow what needs to be dealt with today. Years ago, however, I stumbled on to something that has really worked for me.

I have a private spot in my home where I take the child who needs a talk. We sit facing each other on two comfortable chairs, and we stay there until we resolve the matter. When I first started doing this, it felt a little awkward and difficult; but I saw wonderful fruit from it right away. Now my children tease each other about it. "Oh, you're going for a CHAT with dad, are you?" Yet each one of my children actually likes the process because it works.

David was a loving father who lacked a very important tool in his parental toolkit. I'm glad, though, that the Bible records his miss so that we can learn from it.

Practical Parenting TIPS  *For Today*

Address difficult issues with your children *before* feelings get out of hand. Follow these simple rules for a meaningful "CHAT" with your child:

1. Build your child up and let them know how much you love them.
2. Make sure your child understands that the purpose of the "chat" is to hear, be heard, and to resolve the issue.
3. Tell them what concerns you.
4. Stop talking!
5. Listen. Listen until you understand their perspective.
6. Keep voices calm and tempers in check.
7. No one leaves a "chat" until you resolve the matter.
8. Always end your "chat" by praying together and hugging each other.

CHAPTER 29

David Gets Duped:

Set Honesty as the Only Policy

*W*hen my firstborn was a cute little toddler, she tried a well-known, stay-out-of-trouble device called lying. It's funny how the idea for this device seems to come to children almost naturally. I didn't even think my daughter was old enough to understand what a lie was.

I asked her a simple question, and after a moment's hesitation, I received a simple reply that initially satisfied me. When I turned back to what I was doing, I suddenly knew that she had lied to me. I also instantly knew that God, in his grace, must have shown me this, because it had been the furthest thing from my mind.

My daughter and I had a daughter-sitting-on-dad's-knee chat, and it turned out that while she didn't know linguistically what lying was, she knew it experientially.

As I read the stories of David's family life, I felt amazed at how often his children deceived him and lied to him. They even duped their dad in some of their most hideous plots.

When Amnon wanted to sleep with his half-sister, Tamar, he had a hard time getting her alone. So he pretended to get sick, and when his dad the king came to visit, Amnon asked if his sister could come to care for him. So when David sent his daughter to care for his son, Amnon raped her (2 Samuel 13:1–22).

When Absalom wanted to kill Amnon, he threw a party for all of the king's sons and asked Dad to send them all over. David agreed and so unknowingly sent Amnon to his death (2 Samuel 13:23–29).

It floors me that the Bible never says David did anything about being duped by his own children.

After these two instances, trust seemed to plummet to an all-time low in the royal family. David's affair with Bathsheba, his order to have her husband killed, and all his efforts to hide his tracks became public. God also told David that for using the sword of the Ammonites to kill Uriah, that that sword would never depart from his house.

> *"Why did you despise the word of the LORD by doing what is evil in his eyes? You struck down Uriah the Hittite with the sword and took his wife to be your own. You killed him with the sword of the Ammonites. Now, therefore, the sword will never depart from your house, because you despised me and took the wife of Uriah the Hittite to be your own."* (2 Samuel 12:9–10)

God told David that the same sword of violence and deception that he used would strike time and again against his family line. Sure enough, David's sons not only killed each other and tried to take the throne by force, but they deceived their father and each other in the process.

If you sow deception, your children likely will learn that deception is the way to solve problems and get around obstacles—and sooner or later, you'll be viewed as one of those obstacles.

From the time that I had that toddler-to-father chat with my daughter, I made a family motto about our words that we all try to live by: "If I say it, you can count on it; if I say it, it's the truth."

Unlike David, you must make yourself an example of honesty and faithfulness. And you should never neglect to deal with your children's all-too-natural forays into the realm of little whites and big whoppers. Remember, the strength of our relationships depends on trust—and trust is earned when our words can be believed and relied on.

Practical Parenting TIPS *For Today*

Your children should know that your word is as good as gold and that they can count on it and trust it always. That way, whenever your children say one thing and attempt to do another, you can hold them to their word by asking them if they like it when you keep your promises to them. Your commitment to never lie to them also provides a foundation to work from when they have that I'm-not-sure-that-I-want-to-tell-the-whole-truth look on their face.

CHAPTER 30

The Wisdom of Solomon:

Teaching Your Children to Be Wise

*W*hen I first became a Christian, I heard a preacher recommend that people read one of the thirty-one chapters of the Book of Proverbs on each corresponding day of the month. I read, studied, and meditated on a chapter a day for two or three years, and God used it to transform the way I looked at life, the way I thought, and the way I behaved.

The Book of Proverbs is the only book in the Bible that mentions it was written, in part, to help teach children. Solomon, the author of most of the book, reveals that his father, David, started teaching him while he was very young and teachable (tender) to go after wisdom (Proverbs 4:3–9).

Solomon then advises his own son to seek wisdom and understanding. Solomon went further than his father did, however, and actually wrote out the wisdom that he wanted his son to seek, learn, and apply, in the form of Proverbs.

We have the benefit of having that God-inspired, practical life wisdom to teach to our own children. When I started teaching my children about life, I'd find myself repeatedly reading and quoting from the Book of Proverbs. The years I spent with my nose planted firmly and daily in the Book of Proverbs came in really handy. So I went back to the Bible that I used during that time and opened it up to those familiar and well-marked-up pages, and started going over it again for review and to keep it ready in my heart for teaching my children.

As my children got older, they started reading Proverbs for themselves. Today, the concepts taught in Proverbs have become part of the make-up of my children and help to govern how they live. I've seen firsthand the incredible benefit of following God's prescription for teaching children practical and godly wisdom.

Before we roll up our sleeves and start reading, quoting, and teaching Proverbs, however, we must learn one thing from the parenting example of the guy whom God used to give us this awesome parenting tool. Solomon's own son and successor, Rehoboam, appears in the biblical record as anything but wise.

When Rehoboam became king, his people made an important request of him:

> *"Your father put a heavy yoke on us, but now lighten the harsh labor and the heavy yoke he put on us, and we will serve you."* (1 Kings 12:4)

Rehoboam sent the people away, promising them an answer in three days, and then he talked with his counselors. So far, so good. He remembered his father's wisdom and didn't give a hasty answer, and also sought wise counsel. The older men who had served as Solomon's counselors advised him to lighten the people's burden. His buddies, on the other hand, counseled him to do the opposite. He followed his young friends advice, and after the room had cleared, only one tribe remained for him to rule. God had said that the kingdom would split because of Solomon's backsliding (1 Kings 12:1–22), and he fulfilled his promise in a revealing way.

Rehoboam followed in his dad's backsliding footsteps. We have no record of Rehoboam seeking God's direction in this decision.

Rehoboam was not a very wise king. The Scripture sums up his problem in one sentence: *"He did evil because he had not set his heart on seeking the LORD"* (2 Chronicles 12:14).

Solomon had taught that the fear of the Lord is the beginning of wisdom, yet he himself had turned away from serving God in the later part of his life, leaving his son with only part of the wisdom equation.

Wisdom does not come merely from learning principles and knowledge in the form of proverbs or wise sayings. A person could spend his whole life accumulating knowledge and reading and studying the world's greatest "7 Steps to Success in Life" books, and still not become wise. Wisdom comes from God. It can be found only in relationship with God and in viewing life from his perspective.

The New Testament tells us:

> *If any of you lacks wisdom, he should ask God, who gives generously to all without finding fault, and it will be given to him.* (James 1:5)

James focuses on wisdom coming from God through our relationship with him. God gave us the Book of Proverbs, and he wants us and our children to become familiar with the principles that govern this life, but he doesn't want us to seek wisdom apart from seeking him. Wisdom comes when we ask God to help us understand the principles and how to apply them in each situation. The combination of knowing the principles and then daily seeking God's wisdom for understanding and application is the key.

Rehoboam no doubt knew the principles his father taught, but because he didn't know the God that Solomon sought in his early years, Rehoboam turned out to be anything but wise.

Practical Parenting TIPS *For Today*

Introduce your children to the practical life wisdom taught in the Book of Proverbs by reading a chapter each day for a year. The book has thirty-one chapters, so you can read the chapter that corresponds to each day of the month—this will help you stay on track. This is a great dinner table discussion starter. Read the chapter, but then reread a few verses and ask everyone what they mean and how they can be applied to their lives. Start each session with prayer, sincerely asking God for wisdom (like James said we should), wisdom that grows out of a growing relationship with the Lord.

Two Prophets and Three Mothers:

Everyday Family Miracles

I love reading about Elijah and Elisha, two prophets whom God used to accomplish some marvelous miracles: calling fire down from heaven, conquering enemy armies with the assistance of angelic armies, proclaiming the start and end of famines, outrunning chariots, and much more. In the midst of these mind-boggling acts of God that altered kingdoms, these two prophets also dealt with and talked to God about three mothers.

While the land writhed in a severe drought (which Elijah had announced ahead of time), God told the prophet to visit a widow whom God had commanded to feed him. He found her and asked for food. She replied that she was about to use the last of her oil and flour to make one final meal for her and her son. Elijah had the audacity to ask her to feed him first, but promised that when she did, a miracle would happen.

And it did: the flour and oil never ran out—no matter how much she used—until the drought ended. Later, when this same widow's son died, she took the boy to Elijah, and the prophet prayed and delivered the son alive back to his mother (1 Kings 17).

Fast-forward to Elisha's time and another widow; she came to Elisha, explaining that she had no way to meet her commitments and that creditors were coming to take her two boys as slaves. Elisha told her to borrow as many big, empty jars as she could and to pour into them the oil she kept in a little jar. When she did this, the oil didn't stop flowing until she and her sons ran out of borrowed jars. Then she sold the oil and had enough money to pay her creditors, plus extra to live off of (2 Kings 4).

The third woman was neither a widow nor in need of provision. This married woman of means prepared a private room in her home for Elisha so that he had a place to stay when he traveled. Elisha wanted to reward her kindness and tried to find out what she wanted or needed. Elisha's servant reminded him that she was childless, so Elisha told her that she'd have a son in about a year from that time. She got pregnant, had a son, and one day while he was still young, he died. The distraught woman put her boy on the prophet's bed without telling anyone what had happened and traveled to see the prophet. He came to her home and raised him back to life (2 Kings 4).

While Jesus ministered in his own hometown, he mentioned one of these widows to help explain why he didn't perform any great miracles there, where everyone knew him as Joseph's son.

> *Jesus said to them, "Surely you will quote this proverb*
> *to me: 'Physician, heal yourself! Do here in your home-*
> *town what we have heard that you did in Capernaum.'*
> *"I tell you the truth," he continued, "no prophet is*
> *accepted in his hometown. I assure you that there were*
> *many widows in Israel in Elijah's time, when the sky was*
> *shut for three and a half years and there was a severe*
> *famine throughout the land. Yet Elijah was not sent to*
> *any of them, but to a widow in Zarephath in the region*
> *of Sidon."* (Luke 4:23–26)

Many things get in the way of our faith. Neither the widow whom Jesus mentioned here nor the man he spoke of in his next example was an Israelite. This made the crowd so angry that they drove Jesus out of town and tried to throw him off a cliff (Luke 4:28–30). Sometimes we get so comfortable in our Christian faith and in the way we live, that we forget God is a supernatural God who can provide for us and answer our prayers in a way far beyond our wildest expectation.

The first widow made food for Elijah before she served herself and her son, even though a few minutes earlier she had enough food only for one last meal for her own starving family. God rewarded her demonstration of faith and provided for her during the drought. She continued to feed and house Elijah, and when her son got sick and died—even though she couldn't conceive of such a thing—her son was returned to her from the dead.

The second widow came to the prophet Elisha seeking God's intervention. When she heard his instructions, she followed them to the letter, demonstrating her faith; and her sons not only escaped the clutches of her creditors, but she found her family abundantly provided for.

The third woman approached Elisha without need, but with a desire to help him in doing God's work. Her service demonstrated her faith in God, and the Lord rewarded her with a son. When the son died, she lay his body on the prophet's bed and left to tell the prophet, showing that she knew God could and would take care of her dire situation.

Did you notice that, in each of these cases, the children involved were provided for, cared for, and kept safe? In fact, each instance dealt with the concerns of a mother and her children. The children would have seen their mother's faith and obedience at work, bringing God's grace, power, and help into their homes.

God sent his power through these mighty men of God to change the political map, steer nations, and bring his people back to himself; but he also sent them to establish faith in and help needy families.

So where do we find a mighty prophet of God? Jesus is God's Son, and he lives in us by his Spirit. God is our Father, and as Christians we no longer need a prophet to stand in the gap; we can go directly to him and *"receive mercy and find grace to help us in our time of need"* (Hebrews 4:16).

Many years ago, when things got quite tight financially for our family, we opened our home to another family going through an even tighter time. The few groceries we had got divided carefully before each meal. One day we had enough hot dogs for each child to have one apiece. We prayed together and asked God to make the food we had to be enough. At the end of the meal, two hot dogs remained on the plate. One child asked for another. Her face fell when we carefully explained that we had enough for only one each. Of course, we thought her look showed disappointment, but when she explained that she already had eaten two, we realized it had to be something else. In order to find out who went without, we rounded up all the kids and took a count. They had eaten more hot dogs than we started with—and yet two still remained on the plate!

This was no earth-shattering, life-changing kind of miracle, but my children have never forgotten it. The incident inspired both their faith and their prayer life.

The author of Hebrews wrote:

> *And without faith it is impossible to please God, because anyone who comes to him must believe that he exists and that he rewards those who earnestly seek him.* (Hebrews 11:6)

I love that verse. God not only insists that we believe in him, but he also requires us to believe that he rewards us when we seek him! It's impossible to please God without faith; it's therefore impossible for us to raise children who please God without demonstrating to them faith in action.

Oh, and don't worry about having enough faith to make all this work—taking the first step, just like the three mothers in the previous stories, demonstrates your faith; God will take you from there. A simple prayer over some hot dogs can get the ball rolling.

Practical Parenting TIPS  *For Today*

God doesn't care only about the nations and the church; he cares about your family and he wants to care for you, help you, provide for you, and look after you and your children. Ask him for the things your family needs and trust that he hears you and loves you and will move on your behalf. Pray together around the dinner table, asking God about your needs and the things that concern your family. If you're having trouble believing that God will really move on your behalf, ask him to help you with your faith and to deal with your doubts. Your children (and perhaps you too) will learn the valuable lessons that God is faithful and can be trusted in all things.

CHAPTER 32

Little Kings, Joash and Josiah:

Making the Transition from Your Faith to Theirs

*T*hese days, the term *tweens* often describes kids aged ten to twelve. They're at that "in between" age, when they no longer like being called children but aren't quite ready to be called teens.

From a spiritual standpoint, they're in between Bible stories, bedtime prayers, and personal devotions. It's imperative that we help our tweens make the transition from viewing Christianity as "what my parents teach me" to "what I believe and am committed to."

I believe we can see the importance of this principle by comparing two kids who became kings of Judah during their tween years.

When Joash was a small child, a caring relative hid him away in the temple while his wicked grandmother murdered every male in the family in order to secure the throne for herself. His uncle Jehoiada, a godly priest who taught the young would-be king what he needed to know about serving and following God, raised him.

Jehoiada helped put Joash on the throne, replacing his wicked grandmother when he was just seven years old. He was a good and godly king—for a while, anyway.

> *Joash did what was right in the eyes of the LORD all the years Jehoiada the priest instructed him.*
> (2 Kings 12:2)

> *After the death of Jehoiada, the officials of Judah came and paid homage to the king, and he listened to them. They abandoned the temple of the LORD, the God of their fathers, and worshiped Asherah poles and idols. Because of their guilt, God's anger came upon Judah and Jerusalem."* (2 Chronicles 24:17–18)

The next few verses record that God sent Jehoiada's son to warn Joash, and forgetting his uncle's kindness, Joash murdered his cousin.

And so this boy, raised and advised by his priest uncle, stayed true to God so long as his uncle lived; but as soon as he died, the young king followed the advice of others to move in the opposite direction. He never made a wholehearted decision of his own for the Lord, so when the winds of influence changed direction, he changed with them.

About 150 years later, under very different circumstances, another boy got placed on Judah's throne. Manasseh, Judah's most wicked king, died and left the kingdom to his wicked son, Amon. Amon's officials assassinated him after a reign of only two years. The people got together and killed the assassins, then once more got out the proverbial booster seat and placed Josiah, Amon's eight-year-old son, on the big ruling chair.

So how did this little king fare with such a wicked lineage and no priestly uncle instructing him along the way?

> *Neither before nor after Josiah was there a king like him who turned to the LORD as he did—with all his heart and with all his soul and with all his strength, in accordance with all the Law of Moses.* (2 Kings 23:25)

So how did this happen? The Bible doesn't tell us who influenced Josiah in this godly direction, but it does tell us what happened inside his heart.

> *In the eighth year of his reign, while he was still young, he began to seek the God of his father David.*
> (2 Chronicles 34:3)

A decision to seek God comes from the heart. This young king did not merely follow along with what he was taught or try to do what was right because it was right; instead, he made a heart decision to go after God, to seek God with everything he had and was.

As Christian parents, we must do everything in our power to influence our children to seek the Lord for themselves, not merely to follow along in our church steps. If they're along only for the ride, they will not stay around when something that looks better to them comes along. We need to help our kids take hold of the faith and begin to seek God for themselves.

How do we do that?

First, we need to let them know that being a Christian isn't just about believing and doing all the right things. It's chiefly about having a living, growing relationship with God. Jesus came to die for our sins, not just to forgive them. Jesus died in order to give us the opportunity to be with, get to know, follow, and love and be loved by our awesome heavenly Father, forever. Planting and watering this seed from a young age will steer children toward the time in their life when their faith becomes personal. And it becomes personal only when they start to seek God for themselves.

Second, jumping back to the tween years, it's important that we help our children gradually make the transition from a nightly routine of Bible stories and prayers with us, to them taking ownership of this time on their own. We need to encourage them through this stage, not to just get their devotions done, but to slow down and seek God, listening and desiring to get to know him.

I once heard it said that a parent's job is to hold a child's hand until the time comes to transfer it into God's hand. I would add that, in the tween years, parents need to hold one hand while encouraging their children to let God hold the other.

Practical Parenting TIPS  *For Today*

Remember the steps of **teach, train,** and **mentor** as you help your children build from your faith to a personal faith of their own. For example, don't do everything for them: instead of always telling them what's right or what the Bible says, ask them questions and help them think it out for themselves. As hard as it may be, don't be too quick to rescue your children from problems—instead, steer them to prayer and to God for a solution.

CHAPTER 33

Esther and Mordecai:

Teach Them Not to Sweat (But to Do) the Small Stuff

"His master replied, 'Well done, good and faithful servant! You have been faithful with a few things; I will put you in charge of many things. Come and share your master's happiness.'" (Matthew 25:21)

I learned many years ago that Jesus' admonition to be faithful with a few things didn't only mean that I'd get a bigger load of responsibilities. God will give more to a person who has effectively handled a small amount of responsibility, because in learning to do the little things well, they automatically become equipped to handle bigger things.

If you make your bed when you first get out of it, return anything you use to its designated spot, and deal properly with each piece of clothing as it comes off of your body—all little things—then you will have an easier time keeping a tidy bedroom. Disciplining yourself to rule all those little things, which takes nominal effort, automatically prepares you to rule over a bigger task.

An old Jewish proverb says, "Take care of the pennies and the dollars will take care of themselves." If you make the right decision with small amounts of money, the larger picture of your finances will look rosy—faithful in little, ruler of much.

Life is made up of smaller parts, and the same principles govern them all, regardless of size. So if our children learn to manage a bedroom well, they can go on to manage a home. If they learn how to love their brothers and sisters, they learn the principles that will help them succeed in their adult relationships.

Joseph was a prime example of this. The Bible shows him working hard and being faithful in Potiphar's house. He gained Potiphar's favor and eventually took charge of the whole household. He did the same thing in prison. Then, when it came time to become second in command over all Egypt, he didn't find it a difficult or onerous task, for the principles he had learned about character, relationships, and management as a slave and a prisoner remained the same for running an empire.

Mordecai adopted and raised his relative, Esther, after the death of her parents. When it came time to find the Persian king a new queen, the beautiful young virgins, including Esther, were rounded up and taken to the palace. Esther wowed the socks off of everyone, including the king, and she became his queen. The Bible records the secret of her success. When the eunuch in charge of the harem told her what to do to impress the king, she listened and followed his instructions, just as she had learned to do when she was growing up with Mordecai.

> *When the turn came for Esther (the girl Mordecai had adopted, the daughter of his uncle Abihail) to go to the king, she asked for nothing other than what Hegai, the kings eunuch who was in charge of the harem, suggested. And Esther won the favor of everyone who saw her.* (Esther 2:15, emphasis added)

> *But Esther had kept secret her family background and nationality just as Mordecai had told her to do, for she continued to follow Mordecai's instructions as she had done when he was bringing her up.*
(Esther 2:20, emphasis added)

Esther listened well, learned, and continued to apply what she had learned as an adopted daughter, a harem virgin, and finally as queen.

Mordecai had raised her well, and she continued to follow his instruction. Doing the right thing one step at a time, one little decision at a time, took her to the king's side as queen, and eventually she became the one God would use to rescue the Jewish people from annihilation.

Esther revealed herself as consistently teachable, obedient, polite, humble, responsible, respectful, resourceful, unselfish, decisive, personable, organized, tactful, and wise. Responding to each of life's moments with such godly traits will help you succeed whether you're called to be a nurse, a salesman, or a monarch.

How do you raise someone who could become queen and the most powerful person on the planet? A small but constant flow of water can break and shape stone. As we raise our children, we need to help them understand that consistently doing the right thing in the small situations will help them get where God wants them to be. Help them understand that, as with Esther, God often uses our own right responses to the small things to unfold our destiny.

When Esther faced the most important and difficult decision of her life, Mordecai reminded her of this principle. Mordecai had requested that the queen see the king and ask him to spare the Jews from Haman's planned genocide—but she hesitated, for she knew it was against the law to approach the king uninvited. Unless he spared her, she would die for such an infraction. To complicate things, he hadn't called for her for a month, so she probably felt he had grown unhappy with her. Listen to Mordecai's response to Esther's dilemma:

> *He sent back this answer: "Do not think that because you are in the king's house you alone of all the Jews will escape. For if you remain silent at this time, relief and deliverance for the Jews will arise from another place, but you and your father's family will perish. And who knows but that you have come to royal position for such a time as this?"* (Esther 4:13–14)

Mordecai basically reminded her that a wrong choice never yields the right results, and that wrong choices steer us away from God's plan just as right ones take us toward it.

I opened this chapter with the famous words of Jesus that all Christians want to hear when they stand before God:

"His master replied, 'Well done, good and faithful servant! You have been faithful with a few things; I will put you in charge of many things. Come and share your master's happiness.'" (Matthew 25:21)

The secret to helping your children one day hear those words is found in the verse—help them understand the crucial importance of being faithful in the small things.

Practical Parenting **TIPS** *For Today*

It may seem as though you're sweating the small stuff when you insist that your children not bend the truth, that they obey, that they apologize and make up for the small offenses, etc.. But if you make them understand how their response to the little things steers their lives toward greatness or obscurity, they'll understand that you're doing what's best for them. You may even want to sit your children down and read this chapter with them and discuss how important it is for you to help them get the little things right. After you've talked over this principle, it will be easy to bring them back on track by reminding them of Joseph and Esther.

CHAPTER 34

Job:

Trusting God When Parenting Hurts

While he was still speaking, yet another messenger came and said, "Your sons and daughters were feasting and drinking wine at the oldest brother's house, when suddenly a mighty wind swept in from the desert and struck the four corners of the house. It collapsed on them and they are dead, and I am the only one who has escaped to tell you!" At this, Job got up and tore his robe and shaved his head. Then he fell to the ground in worship and said: "Naked I came from my mother's womb, and naked I will depart. The LORD gave and the LORD has taken away; may the name of the LORD be praised." In all this, Job did not sin by charging God with wrongdoing. (Job 1:18–22)

Job suffered enormous pain as a parent, losing all ten of his children in one tragic day. Pain in parenting can come from quite a few directions: some lose their children, as Job did;

others have to watch as their children suffer prolonged sickness or disease, or as they struggle with some handicap or deformity; and still others endure great pain when a child rebels and makes wrong choices or turns her heart away from them. However the pain comes, it can feel excruciating and impossibly hard to bear.

When Job's friends arrived to comfort him, they ended up doing anything but that. They waxed poetic for chapter after chapter, trying to convince Job that bad things happen to bad people and that good things happen to good people. At one point, one of his friends seemed to concede that, just maybe, Job's children died because of their own sin; but the general thrust of their arguments put Job in the blame spotlight.

At the end of the book, God told Job's friends that they had it all wrong. What happened to Job's children was not his fault, nor did it happen because he sinned.

When something bad happens to our children, one of the first things we want to do is level blame—and we often level the blame gun at ourselves. Although Job wanted an answer and an accounting from God, he didn't blame himself or God, or anyone else, for that matter. Some things just *are* and no one is to blame. Even when someone is to blame, dwelling on it won't take away the pain or fix the problem.

Ultimately, we go through the blame stage of grief because we are really like Job; we want to know *why*. Why me? Why my kids? Why did it happen? Why does it have to be this way? How could God allow this to happen?

After Job's friends finally put a sock in it, God spoke directly to Job. God asked him a ton of questions, which can be loosely summed up like this: Were you there when I made everything? Do you understand why I made each thing, what purpose it has, and how it works? And can you change or alter the purposes that I have set in place?

God told Job that he was seeking to understand something far beyond his ability to comprehend. Nevertheless, he should take comfort in knowing that God remains faithful and able and that his actions never conflict with his plans and purposes.

There is nothing wrong with seeking to understand "why" when something goes wrong. The Bible is full of examples of people who sought understanding and got it. Sometimes, however, the things that happen lay beyond our ability to understand; and when that happens, we must ask God to give us the ability to trust him, even though we don't understand.

The Bible tells us that trouble comes for many reasons. For one thing, we live in a fallen world full of sinful people, so we get exposed to the tragedy and pain that comes with that. It also explains that the devil roams the planet, seeking to steal, kill, and destroy. We also reap what we sow, for both good and bad. And if all that weren't enough, it also teaches that God tests our faith, disciplines us for our own good, and that we *will* suffer for standing up for and sharing our faith.

When trouble strikes and we struggle with a tangle of emotions, it can be difficult to discern which of these factors (or combinations thereof) apply. We need to remember that God is good and trustworthy, and that if we trust him, then no matter what we face or why, he'll walk through it with us. Sometimes, during a painful time, our view of God can get skewed. Remind yourself that God is not up in heaven unaware or unconcerned about what you are suffering. He's also not in the path in front of you, throwing obstacles in your way to see how you'll respond.

As Christians, we are God's children, and he's promised to live in us and to walk with us. He's promised that he'll never leave us nor forsake us and that we can rely on him whenever we need his help. God walks with us and beside us, helping us work through, deal with, and conquer whatever gets in our path, no matter how it got there or why.

If tragedy strikes or things aren't the way you think they should be, remember that God is there for you, on your side, ready to comfort you and get you through it.

Practical Parenting TIPS *For Today*

If your children are sick, hurt, or in trouble, you can reflect later if necessary on the why; but the first thing out of your mouth should be a heartfelt request for help from the only One who loves them even more than you do. When our faith gets tested, we need to draw closer to God and trust him even more— that's how you get an A on the test. If you're having trouble hanging on, ask God to help you trust him. Once when a man asked Jesus to rescue his child "if" he could, Jesus replied, "If you can? All things are possible to him who believes." What came next should fill every parent with hope—the man replied, "I do believe; help me overcome my unbelief." In other words, he said, "I choose to believe, but I'm having trouble; please help me." The man's son was healed! God loves you and your children. He wants to help and he'll even help you to trust him (Mark 9:19–27).

CHAPTER 35

Song of Songs:

The Sex Talk

The Song of Songs is one of the most loved, but also one of the most controversial, books in the Bible. Much loved because of its beautiful poetry, wonderful language, and vivid and passionate love story imagery; very controversial, for basically the same reason. The controversy seems to come down to the way the book gets interpreted and the reason it was included in the Bible.

Many scholars have concluded that the book is a romantic and ardent love story meant to celebrate and inspire married love. Others feel it gives us glimpses into the wonderful mysteries of Christ and the church.

Paul follows both tracks in the Book of Ephesians. The parallels between marital love and the relationship between Christ and the church seem so evident to Paul that he feels completely comfortable teaching about them both, simultaneously.

In this same way, husbands ought to love their wives as their own bodies. He who loves his wife loves himself. After all, no one ever hated his own body, but he feeds and cares for it, just as Christ does the church—for we are members of his body. "For this reason a man will leave his father and mother and be united to his wife, and the two will become one flesh." This is a profound mystery—but I am talking about Christ and the church. However, each one of you also must love his wife as he loves himself, and the wife must respect her husband. (Ephesians 5:28–33)

The title *Song of Songs* means the ultimate song, just like "King of kings" refers to the ultimate King, or the King to whom all other kings will bow down. When you recognize the dual interpretation, it's easy to understand the title. This is a song that celebrates not only the greatest gifts of life—relationship with God and relationship with others—but specifically rejoices over the two highest forms of these gifts: married love and the loving relationship between Christ and the church.

Having said all of this, I see the Song of Songs as an awesome parenting tool. The love story is not about two people married for years, but about two young people who fall deeply in love and end up getting married. If the book is meant to inspire and direct young love, leading up to, during, and after the wedding night, wouldn't it be an ideal tool to help parents guide would-be lovers in the right direction?

The Song of Songs is great for a number of different reasons. First, the book contains God's words and viewpoint. Second, the book doesn't deal with the topic in a prudish manner, but with a wonderful balance hard to find when abstinence becomes the main focus for our little talks. It openly rejoices over married love—in the heart, the mind, and with the body—all the while keeping it in the context of marriage.

Reading through the Song of Songs with your preteen or teenager can open up all kinds of conversation. Just start talking about what each of you thinks the words and metaphors refer to and what God's purpose for the text might be. It's like "the sex talk" concentrate—just add conversation and stir.

The book offers many valuable conversation starters and lessons. Three times, for example, the reader is admonished to not, *"arouse or awaken love until it so desires,"* helping us teach our children that God created a proper progression for love. Some things should take place before, and others not until after, the wedding. Helping them understand this will assist them in avoiding situations prone to starting the sexual ball rolling before the right time.

In the book, the betrothed, and then married couple focus all of their sensual desires and imaginations on each other—remaining faithful in heart as well as in deed. We can use this to help our children steer their youthful imaginations to their wedding night and the marriage bed only. We must help them steer their thoughts.

Even the fact that the book includes questions and responses from friends and onlookers helps us teach our children that what we do with our bodies is not just between us and the one we desire. What we do affects our families and our communities; we need to be held accountable by others.

The love described in the Song of Songs grows in the heart, and when the time is right, gets expressed with the body. It's committed as well as passionate, and perseveres through the tough times. The book suggests many topics of discussion, and because of the way its written, you can go only as far as your child needs. For example, its descriptions of the sexual relationship can help you in discussing some "How To" tips at the right time. How far you go with that depends on how close they are to their wedding night.

We can also use the allegorical view to teach our children how the marriage relationship mirrors the relationship between Christ and the church. Compare these verses with what Paul taught in Ephesians 5.

I suggest that you read the book over several times, and possibly get commentary (or at least an introduction to the book) before diving in. The preparation won't take long, but it'll help you lead the discussion and make it more productive.

The Bible talks about sex as a great and wonderful gift, but it also issues strong warnings against its misuse. These warnings don't exist because God is a cosmic killjoy, but because he created everything and he knows how it's meant to work. So he encourages us toward what will bring us happiness and steers us away from what will bring us sorrow. Our children need to be led through the minefield of our culture's misinformation and then pointed beyond it to God's best for them and their marriage. And the greatest of all "Songs" is there to help.

Practical Parenting
TIPS  *For Today*

In our culture, the topic of sex is no longer taboo; it's often the main topic. If we don't actively engage our children in conversation about God's purpose for and view of sex, the world around us will fill the void quickly and incorrectly. It is our responsibility to actively help, shape, and guard our children's attitudes toward sex and marriage, using a biblical world view. Read the Song of Songs and arm yourself with other resources that will help you explain God's purpose and instruction regarding sex. Some really good materials are available from your local Christian bookstore for your kids to read for themselves.

Even though we know how important this topic is, it often gets shuffled to the bottom of our priority list. Why? Often because we all feel a little uneasy, or perhaps embarrassed, about talking to our kids about it. If you feel this way, pray and ask God for his wisdom and timing to open a natural opportunity for the conversation.

CHAPTER 36

Daniel at School:

What to Do About What They Learn

 $\mathcal{D}$ aniel's life and the details surrounding it fascinate me. This man of God, full of deep integrity and wisdom, wrote some of the most detailed and much-studied prophecies in the Bible.

As a teenager, Daniel was uprooted from his home and taken as a captive to Babylon. He ended up in the royal court after the king ordered several young Israelite captives of noble birth to be brought to the palace (Daniel 1:3). Until the time Daniel was taken captive, he evidently grew up in either the royal family or in a very influential home.

Daniel was a young boy when the very godly Josiah ruled Judah. So since Daniel probably grew up in an influential family during Josiah's reign, he likely was raised with spiritual training and with a godly world view.

Daniel and three other teenage Israelites were taken to the king's court to get a Babylonian education. All four of the boys received Babylonian names. Daniel was called Belteshazzar; the name hints at the purpose of his education. "El" at the end of Daniel's Hebrew name refers to God. "Bel" at the beginning of his new name referred to a Babylonian god. Daniel and his friends were to be educated not only in regular school topics like literature, but they were to be trained to think and view the world, in every way, as the Babylonians did.

In other words, they attended a school similar to those where many Christians send their children to get educated today. Our public schools don't only strive to give children a God-neutral education; very often they contradict what Christians believe.

Some contend that it's our job to stand up, be counted, and change all of this. I wouldn't disagree, but I'd like to point out something even more fundamental: it's not the governments job to ensure that our children get the right intellectual or spiritual education—that's *our* job. Government schooling should aid us in getting the job done, of course, but when we recognize the task as ours, we no longer resign ourselves to the status quo, but instead do what we can to fill in the gaps and right the wrongs in our own child's education.

If your child is gifted in music, for example, you may conclude that the music program at her school is just not enough. So what do you do? You take control and get her involved in lessons outside of school.

In the same way, if your children attend public school and are being taught things contrary to the truth, then it's your responsibility to fix the problem. You may consider it a civic responsibility to help change things on a political level, but while you're doing that, it's also your parental responsibility to change it for your child, whether it changes for everyone else or not.

Fortunately, Daniel and his three friends had been well educated in Judah before their exile to Babylon. Not only had they learned what was right, but they also learned (at the very least from what Josiah did) about the dangers of the pagan religions that Josiah worked so hard to eradicate. This would have prepared the four young men to learn, discern, and understand everything they were taught in light of God's truth.

In Babylon they learned about practices God had forbidden, such as astrology and divination. They didn't refuse to learn about these subjects, but they did recognize them for what they were and refused to practice them. When it came to interpreting dreams or predicting the future, Daniel didn't follow the ways of the Babylonian magicians; he went to God.

We need to prepare our children by educating them in the truth so that when their instructors teach something wrong, they know it and know what the real truth is.

Does this sound like a ton of work that you don't feel equipped to take on? Don't worry; you can do some pretty simple things to make sure you're fulfilling the crucial task of educating your child to view the world from a Christian perspective.

Before diving in to what you can do if your children attend public school, let me briefly speak of the alternatives. Many Christian families are opting to home-school their children, especially in the early years. This is a great idea, but not for everyone, or even possible for everyone. If you go this direction, you'll still need to make sure you get curriculum that features a Christian world view, and also spend time teaching them about what the world around them believes and how to separate truth from error so that they are well prepared to live and believe in the real world.

The other alternative is a Christian school. Again, this is not the right choice for every family, nor is it possible or even available to all. If it is possible and a good Christian school is available to you, it can be a great option.

Just because it's a Christian school, however, doesn't mean that you'll like everything it teaches. If you choose this option, view it as a great assist; but just as you can't delegate spiritual training to the church, so you can't delegate education *carte blanche* to your child's school—whether public or private.

Daniel and his friends arrived in Babylon ready to serve God and to learn in a secular, pagan world. Perhaps their parents believed what Jeremiah (who began his ministry right around the time Daniel was born) prophesied about the exile, and prepared their children for the inevitable. Perhaps they were just protecting them from being led astray by the pagan Canaanite religions. Either way, it's a good thing they did. Daniel changed the world—and all because he was able to chew on what he was taught, compare it with God's truth, and spit out the bones.

Chapter 1 of Daniel records one of the most fascinating details of his story. It describes what happened when Daniel and his friends were tested by the king himself, and also shows what can happen when students trust God and learn through God-colored glasses:

In every matter of wisdom and understanding about which the king questioned them, he found them ten times better than all the magicians and enchanters in his whole kingdom. (Daniel 1:20)

Practical Parenting
TIPS   *For Today*

No matter what schooling option you've chosen, it is important that you add faith to your child's education.

1. Set the foundation for the process; have a discussion with your children, letting them know that what they learn in school may not include a Christian perspective, and that it's part of your job to help them learn that. Ask for their help; ask them to come to you when they wonder about something or when they think that some teaching may contradict their faith. Also train them to openly respond when you ask the dreaded question, "What did you learn in school today?" The question has a purpose.

2. In every way that fits your family and is open to you, make sure your children are growing in the knowledge of their faith and God's Word. The best way to train cashiers to recognize a counterfeit bill is to have them become intimately familiar with the real bills.

3. Teach your children to think things through by asking good questions and letting the conversation flow. That way, when they get to a certain age, like Daniel, they can learn and compare what they learn with what they know of God's Word.

CHAPTER 37

Shadrach, Meshach, and in the Fire You Go:

Peer Proofing

*O*ne thing you can say for sure about King Nebuchadnezzar: he definitely had a flair for the dramatic.

The hot-tempered king set up a ninety-foot-high gold statue and proclaimed that anyone who didn't bow down to it when the music played would be thrown alive into a fiery furnace. When Shadrach, Meshach, and Abednego refused to bow down, the king tossed them into the flames—but after God rescued them from the fire unharmed, Nebuchadnezzar pronounced that anyone who said anything against their God would be cut into pieces and their homes turned into piles of rubble.

Shadrach, Meshach, and Abednego won a great victory of faith that day because they had learned how to stand up to social and cultural pressure to conform or compromise. This, of course, is commonly known today as "peer pressure."

More than likely, these three Hebrews, along with Daniel, were the only people of faith in the whole palace. They faced pressure to conform and compromise from their new government, from the teachers and administrators of their school, and from their fellow students. Yet right from the start they refused to conform—and it's a good thing they made such a decision, because all their lives they continued to feel pressure to cave in. If they were to get it right over a lifetime, they had to make a decision to follow God every day.

When soldiers first took the teens to the palace, the friends were assigned food and wine from the king's table. Although the Bible does not specify the problem with the food, it obviously did not conform to Old Testament dietary laws, so the Hebrew teenagers made a stand. Daniel asked if he and his friends could be fed only vegetables and water. God caused the guy in charge to like Daniel, but he worried that if he didn't feed them properly, the king would have his head. So Daniel proposed a ten-day test. If they looked healthy at the end of the test, then they could continue to eat their modified diet—if not, then they would eat what everyone else did. Ten days later they looked better than the rest of the students, and they got to stick with their kosher menu.

Daniel and his friends having to stand up to cultural and social pressure to compromise became a recurring theme in their lives, as it does for anyone growing up and living in a secular culture. Shortly afterwards, Shad, Mesh, and Abed refused to bow down and worship the ninety-foot-high Oscar (in my imagination, that's what Nebuchadnezzar's statue looked like). Their fellow officials (peers) ran and tattled to the king, who fired up the furnace.

Many years later, Daniel's peers tried to get rid of him by getting the king to sign a law that forbade anyone to pray, except to the king, for thirty days. Again, Daniel refused to compromise, and for his faithfulness to God he got thrown into the lions' den. Yet the lions did not hurt him, just as the fire did not hurt his three friends so long before.

How can we teach our children to remain strong and resist the pressure, no matter who it comes from and why? For some clues, let's look to what we know of these men when they were boys.

They grew up when King Josiah was doing his best to get Judah to serve only God, without compromise. Josiah destroyed idols and pagan worship places all over Judah, and killed the priests and propagators of falsehood. He repaired the temple and restored regular worship and sacrifice. During the repairs to the temple, someone discovered the Book of the Law. Josiah felt horrified when he heard its words, for it predicted exactly what would happen to the nation if it ever forgot to serve God alone without compromise. Josiah gathered the people and had the Law read to them so they could see this for themselves and then decide to compromise no more.

The people rededicated themselves to God and Josiah re-instituted the Passover, celebrating the nation's deliverance from slavery in Egypt. Our four Hebrew heroes of Babylon were born right around the time that Josiah heard the Law and rededicated himself and his nation to living it. And part of living it, of course, included teaching it to their children.

I find God's grace and timing in all of this wonderfully amazing. God had decided that he must send his people into captivity in order to get them to listen and to purify them of the idol worship that had infected their culture. Just before the exile, God raised up Josiah and helped him rid the land of paganism, become familiar with the Law, and lead the people to spiritual rededication.

God knew this wouldn't stick long-term, of course, because his people had gone too far; and sure enough, when Josiah died, they immediately fell back into their old sins. But the really cool thing is that many in Daniels generation grew up experiencing, seeing and hearing of what Josiah did, and it was *that* generation that went to Babylon. Time had run out for the current generation, but God used Josiah to rescue the next by preparing some of them to live and serve God without compromise in Babylon.

God strengthened, prepared, and taught these four young men to live in a pagan world—and even among compromisers of their own people—without wavering. What were the keys? They heard and saw what happened to those who compromise. They knew that their people had landed in Babylon because of it. They had a passionate example of someone who refused to cave in to pressure, probably in their parents and in King Josiah, who as a teenager started to seek God and serve him with all of his heart (2 Chronicles 34:3).

Simply put, they knew where both paths led—and that's what we need to communicate to our children.

Paul warned against remaining ignorant of the devils schemes. Satan's number one tool is the lie. Peer pressure doesn't defeat people nearly as often as the lies that get neatly packaged with it: "You're not hurting anyone," or "Hey, it's your own body," or "God understands that were not perfect," or "It's not really a sin if . . ." These and many other's supply the trip lines that cause our children to fall. At the heart of every one of these lies is the falsehood that if you don't compromise, you'll lose something. Our children need to clearly understand that when you compromise, you lose every time. Only when you do it God's way do you come out ahead.

When Shadrach, Meshach, and Abednego faced the furnace, they knew exactly where they stood on the issue of compromising with the world; that's what gave them strength.

> *Shadrach, Meshach and Abednego replied to the king, "O Nebuchadnezzar, we do not need to defend ourselves before you in this matter. If we are thrown into the blazing furnace, the God we serve is able to save us from it, and he will rescue us from your hand, O king. But even if he does not, we want you to know, O king, that we will not serve your gods or worship the image of gold you have set up."* (Daniel 3:16–18)

The young men didn't compromise. And neither did they burn.

Practical Parenting
TIPS *For Today*

Talk with your children about compromise, peer pressure, and sin. Use the stories in Daniel as a jumping-off point, and then open up the conversation. Keep the conversations going, from time to time, when you speak with them at the end of the day. Just as Shadrach, Meshach, and Abednego supported one another, make an agreement in your family to support each other in your commitment to not compromise. Tell your children age-appropriate stories from your life or the lives of others that clearly demonstrate that compromise means losing and standing firm means winning. Also, be the best example possible and live what you believe, right where your children can see—especially when it's tough.

CHAPTER 38

The Two Messengers, Malachi and John:

Turning Your Heart to Your Children

> "See, I will send you the prophet Elijah before that great and dreadful day of the LORD comes. He will turn the hearts of the fathers to their children, and the hearts of the children to their fathers; or else I will come and strike the land with a curse. (Malachi 4:5–6)

*W*ith these dark verses the Old Testament comes to a close. Since everything in God's Word is there by design and for a reason, what is the purpose for ending with these scary words?

Malachi speaks of two comings: one of the prophet Elijah (John the Baptist) and one of the Lord (Christ).

The angel Gabriel and Jesus both stated that the prophet Malachi referred to John the Baptist (Luke 1:17; Matthew 17:12). John, the first of God's cast of New Testament characters to appear in public ministry, also confirmed that he was the one Malachi predicted.

The name Malachi means "messenger," or "God's messenger," and the first time Malachi prophesied about John (Malachi 3:1), he called him God's messenger. The book of Malachi reads like a sermon guide for John. We see many parallels between the two messengers. They both preached a "rubber meets the road" kind of faith—loving God and loving other's practically. They both talked about honoring God with finances. They both rebuked the religious leaders of their time for not following God in their hearts. They both called for repentance and change. They both announced God's impending judgment on those who refused to turn.

And they both pointed to Jesus.

These two messengers bridge the gap between the two Testaments, concluding one phase of God's plan and showing us what the Lord would carry forward and include in the next.

But how did John fulfill the last words of Malachis prophecy? What did it mean to *"turn the hearts of the fathers to their children, and the hearts of the children to their fathers"*? What message did Malachi carry over the bridge from the Old into the New?

We have no record of John instructing parents about their children or children about their parents. Nor do we have any record of him trying to restore parent/child relationships—so much for a very literal translation.

But before I go further, let me make a disclaimer. The Bible never explains the exact meaning of these verses; therefore anyone who attempts an interpretation must do so humbly. For the reasons I'm about to state, I have my own convictions about God's purpose for these verses. Read carefully, study it for yourself, and see if you agree.

The idea of teaching our children carefully and thoroughly about God and how he wants us to live is very dear to God's heart and provides a key to the working out of his plan. When the Israelites failed to pass their faith on to the next generation, the nation began to slide away from God. When they successfully sought God and taught their children to do the same, the nation of Israel surged forward.

God instructed Abraham to teach his children after him to follow God, so that his descendants could enjoy the blessings of the promise. That promise, of course, was that all nations on earth would be blessed through Abraham's seed, Christ.

When Moses summed up the Law before the Israelites entered the Promised Land, he told them to be sure that they served God, didn't forget God, and that they taught their children how to follow God.

Again, it's no big mystery why—we all die and the next generation moves onto the stage. God created us to learn about him and grow up learning his ways as children. So if parents teach their children properly, then each generation will know his love, grow stronger than the last, and advance God's plan.

Now, listen to the verse in Malachi that comes just before the two in question:

*"Remember the law of my servant Moses, the decrees
and laws I gave him at Horeb for all Israel."*
(Malachi 4:4)

The Old Testament begins to wrap up with one final
reminder to serve and follow God. The next verse tells the
Israelites what to expect next:

*"See, I will send you the prophet Elijah before that
great and dreadful day of the LORD comes."*

Malachi reminds his people to serve God, gives them a
heads-up about the coming Messiah and his messenger, and in
verse 6 then delivers an important note about the messenger:

*"He will turn the hearts of the fathers to their chil-
dren, and the hearts of the children to their fathers; or
else I will come and strike the land with a curse."*

Could it be as simple as God reiterating three things that
needed to be bridged during the four hundred years between
the Old Testament and the New Testament: love and follow
God; look for his salvation in Christ; and pass your faith on
to your children?

This explanation also makes sense in light of the final words
of Malachi: *"or else I will come and strike the land with a curse."*
All the way through the Old Testament, God threatened the
Israelites with a curse if they stopped serving him. Whenever
they failed to teach their children, the next generation fell away
and the curse came.

When the angel Gabriel quoted Malachi to John's father,
Zechariah, he didn't quote it all, and he joined what he did
quote with his own (or God's) words:

> *"And he* [John] *will go on before the Lord, in the spirit and power of Elijah, to turn the hearts of the fathers to their children and the disobedient to the wisdom of the righteous—to make ready a people prepared for the Lord."* (Luke 1:17, parenthesis added)

Although God has always intended to bring all nations back to himself, in the Old Testament, his plan focused on the Israelites. Therefore, for their part, the Israelites needed to have godly children and teach them to love God. In the New Testament, we are called to train our children in godliness *and* to reach out to the lost with the gospel. It seems as though God, through Gabriel, summed up these key points in God's evangelistic plan: *"to turn the hearts of the fathers to their children and the disobedient to the wisdom of the righteous."* Get the parents teaching their children, and call the lost to repentance.

God calls us to live for something beyond ourselves and our generation. We are part of a bigger plan—God's plan to build his kingdom and bring the gospel to the lost. The writer of Hebrews said that Abraham obeyed God because of God's promises, yet he died without ever seeing them fulfilled. Preparing the next generation, despite the cost and effort, is our primary responsibility as Christian parents.

What do you think of this explanation of the last few divinely placed verses of the Old Testament? Could teaching our children really be *that* eternally and theologically important?

Yes, it can.

As we move to the New Testament, we walk across the bridge from Malachi to John the Baptist, carrying with us the message that obeying God and reaching out to others is only half the chore. Teaching the next generation to do the same is the other half.

Practical Parenting TIPS *For Today*

We've covered the "bring your children up in the faith" ground a few times. When God's Word repeats itself and continually hammers home a point, it does so for a purpose—God is trying to show us how important to him, to us, to our children, and to his kingdom this point is. If you haven't started consistently teaching your children God's Word, begun helping them grow in a relationship with God, and helping them live their lives accordingly—or perhaps you have, but you know that God is calling you to do more—then put this book aside for a few moments and pray. Ask God for his help to find the time, overcome the obstacles, and get started. Then grab a pen and piece of paper and write down what you're going to do tomorrow to get you and your family moving in the right direction. Don't get befuddled by the size of the task or the roadblocks or even your own inadequacies. God is with you *right now* and he wants to help. He knows the path through all of your concerns. Just commit it all to him and take the first step. He'll see you through to the next one.

PART TWO

THE NEW TESTAMENT: THE RESULTS OF PARENTING BY THE BOOK

CHAPTER 39

Rejoicing at the Birth of a Baptist:

Helping Your Child Be a Joy and Delight

> *But the angel said to him: "Do not be afraid, Zechariah; your prayer has been heard. Your wife Elizabeth will bear you a son, and you are to give him the name John. **He will be a joy and delight to you, and many will rejoice because of his birth.**"* (Luke 1:13–14, emphasis added)

The angel Gabriel visited Zechariah in order to announce the birth of the last and greatest Old Testament prophet—and the first thing the angel said about the boy is that he'd be a joy and a delight to his parents.

The godly Zechariah and his wife had never had children. It's clear that one of the reasons God chose them to be the parents of John the Baptist is that he wanted to bless them.

Gabriel specifically let Zechariah know that his prayers for a son had been answered.

There were so many priests in Zechariah's day that each one had only a single opportunity to perform the tasks Zechariah was doing that day in the temple. That day may have been the biggest moment in Zechariah's career, and God chose that special moment to announce John's birth. Many priests got the privilege to serve in the temple, but no others that we know of came out with an amazing report of a supernatural visitation. God made John's birth announcement not only important, but special for Zechariah.

The angel also told the old priest that many would rejoice over the birth of his son. Later, when neighbors and relatives heard about John's birth, Luke records that they shared Elizabeth's joy.

The birth announcement was special, the birth was special, and on the eighth day, friends and neighbors gathered to celebrate John's circumcision and his naming. We do not have any record of John's childhood, but the angel had said that he'd be a "joy and delight" to his parents, so it's safe to say that his childhood blessed his parents more than it made them struggle.

Children also become a joy and a delight to their parents by growing up well and making their parents proud. John was a very godly and righteous man, respected by all, and turned out to be a great prophet and messenger for God.

So was this a one-time blessing specifically for John's parents? Or can we learn something from God's Word and see our children become a joy and delight? Wouldn't you like to rejoice over the circumstances of your child's birth, have him

214 REJOICING AT THE BIRTH OF A BAPTIST

be a joy and delight to you throughout his childhood, and
have him turn out wonderful and change the world for God's
kingdom? Let me assume your answer is yes, and proceed.

God meant for parenting to be a wonderful blessing and
each child to be a joy and delight. But we need to follow God
in our parenting and do things the way he meant them to be
done in order for his blessings to follow. Zechariah and his
wife weren't chosen randomly, and the "joy and delight"
promise was not issued as a random one-of-a-kind blessing.
God chose them because they were godly and devout. God no
doubt had prepared them for this task, just as he spent long
years preparing Abraham and Sarah and other great parents
who had preceded John's mom and dad.

As a priest, Zechariah would have known God's Word well.
He probably recognized the angel's announcement as a parenting instruction as much as a parental blessing. Here's what
the Old Testament says about a child being a "joy and
delight."

> *A wise son brings joy to his father, but a foolish son
> grief to his mother.* (Proverbs 10:1)

> *My son, if your heart is wise, then my heart will be
> glad; my inmost being will rejoice when your lips speak
> what is right.* (Proverbs 23:15–16)

> *The father of a righteous man has great joy; he who
> has a wise son delights in him. May your father and
> mother be glad; may she who gave you birth rejoice!*
> (Proverbs 23:24–25)

Discipline your son, and he will give you peace; he will bring delight to your soul. (Proverbs 29:17)

The "joy and delight" blessing comes when you raise your children God's way. Most of the time, children follow what they are taught. If you teach and train your children how to obey, you'll likely be blessed with obedient children. Teach them how to get along with others, and you'll likely be blessed with peace and cooperation in your home. Teach them how to work hard, and you'll likely be blessed with helpful children. Teach them how to seek and follow God, and you'll likely be blessed with godly children. Teach them how to look to God and his Word for wisdom, and you'll likely be blessed with children who make choices that bring you joy and delight.

We all know families, of course, in which the children did *not* follow in the footsteps of their parents' teaching. Generally, however, children will come back to: 1) what they've been taught, and 2) what was expected of them.

I believe that Zechariah realized John was going to be a joy and delight because he and his wife were to give him "joy and delight" instruction—teaching him God's Word and principles and training and disciplining him to live them out.

I also wonder, though, if John's parents let him know what the angel had said about him being a "joy and delight" as an encouragement, helping him move in that direction. Praising your child and letting her know when she's done well, made you proud, and brought you joy and delight can be a powerful motivator.

An angel may not have shown up on your doorstep to personally give you this promise, but you have the same biblical principles and teaching that Zechariah used to make it come to pass.

Make a habit of letting your children know what a blessing it is to be their parent, how much you love them just for being them, and how glad you are to have them in your life. A grateful parent motivates a joyful child!

> *Sons are a heritage from the LORD, children a reward from him." (Psalm 127:3)*

Practical Parenting **TIPS** *For Today*

Here are a few ways you can celebrate your child being a "joy and delight" and encourage them to continue being just that.

1. Remember that being a joy and delight to you should first and foremost be linked to the fact that they're yours and that you love them.

2. Let them know that part of your job as a parent is to help them be a walking "joy and delight" bringer. They should understand that each of us should strive to be a blessing. Help them imagine that when they come into a room, the people who see them should see a blessing walking in: helpful, pleasant, caring, wise, funny, etc.

3. Whenever they bring you joy or delight, or you see them bringing it to others, tell them, praise them, and encourage them on.

CHAPTER 40

Mary and Gabriel Chat:

God's Will For the Timing and Gender of Your Children

*H*aving children was the last thing on Mary's mind when the angel Gabriel showed up and announced her miraculous pregnancy. By that time she was probably a young teenager, and although she was already engaged, her marriage may yet have been some time off.

When Gabriel told her that she was going to have a baby, she had an interesting response: *"How will this be, 'Mary asked the angel,' since I am a virgin?"* (Luke 1:34).

Given Mary's Jewish upbringing, it is likely that she suspected Gabriel was talking about this baby being the Messiah. It was common in Mary's time for girls to be raised with the idea that they could become the mother of the Messiah. Mary, like other girls, would have been taught what the Scriptures say about the Messiah's birth and the details surrounding the other special births in the Old Testament. Mary's first and most obvious clue that this could be a special birth was the appearance of the angel.

The second clue came with the angel's words, "God is with you," which she may have connected with Isaiah's prophecy that the Messiah would be called, "Immanuel", which means "God with us."

> *Therefore the Lord himself will give you a sign: The virgin will be with child and will give birth to a son, and will call him Immanuel.* (Isaiah 7:14)

Mary's response reflects much of what she had learned from the example of Old Testament mothers:

> *"I am the Lord's servant," Mary answered. "May it be to me as you have said." Then the angel left her.*
> (Luke 1:38)

Mary, like Hannah long before her, used the word *servant* to describe herself. It's the absence of any further questions or objections, however, that really demonstrates what Mary had learned and taken to heart. She didn't ask, "But how will I explain this to my parents and to Joseph?" or complain that the timing could cause her to lose Joseph and possibly get stoned to death for adultery. She didn't complain about her age or that her youth was being taken from her, and she didn't grumble that she was about to be loaded down with a huge responsibility that she felt too young to handle.

With his final words, Gabriel may have cut short any

further questions and reminded her to recall all that she'd been taught. He told her:

"For nothing is impossible with God." (Luke 1:37)

These words not only answered her question about how she would get pregnant, but also may have brought Sarah to mind. When the Lord heard Sarah having a chuckle about having a baby in her old age, she was asked, *"Is anything too hard for the LORD?"* (Genesis 18:14).

Mary knew from Sarah's story that God could and would do whatever he said he would do. She knew from the stories of Sarah, Rebekah, Rachel, and Hannah that God's timing is not our timing, yet when we trust him, it's always perfect.

Mary learned from all of the Old Testament stories that she could trust God to know what was best for her and for her children, and that included the timing of their arrival. She completely yielded herself, her plans, her life, and the lives of her children, into God's careful, loving, and faithful hands.

Immediately after my wife and I drove away from our wedding reception, I held her hand and prayed with her that God would give us children at the right time and in his time. We both trusted that God heard our prayer and decided that we would pray and talk about children again each year on our anniversary.

On our fourth anniversary we brought the topic up, and both of us knew in our hearts (before we talked) that the time was right—and approximately nine months later, our first child was born. We continued trusting, praying, and talking about each child. We had three, all approximately three years apart, and each time we both knew that the time was right.

Everything about the arrival of our children and their birth order, and their gender (all of which we prayed about and left in God's hands), was wonderfully perfect for us and our family.

We must put every detail concerning the timing, gender, and number of our children into God's care and trust him, as he calls us to do in every area of our lives. Only God can see how every detail and decision affects our future and the future and eternity of others. We should not bring children into this world aided by our wisdom alone.

Yes, God wants us to use wisdom, but always in submission to his will. There's nothing wrong with using wisdom to plan your family and following sensible advice like, "Don't have children right away when you're first married," "Don't have your children too close together," and "Don't have more than you can properly love and train." Like Mary and those who mentored her, we need to hold this practical wisdom loosely as a starting point and submit it to God's will and plan.

Also, remember that God is bigger and that his love for each child is bigger than our ability to sort everything out. He turns "accidents" into providence. God wants to partner with us, and the best way is always to do things his way. We suffer and bring hardship on others when we do things our own way and expect God to just work it all out.

Do you want to do things God's way in regard to the timing and gender of your children? If so, the first step is to submit to God's straightforward truth. No child, for example, is meant to be conceived prior to a wedding. If you're having sex prior to the "I do," then you're playing Russian Roulette with God's plan for you and his plan for the next generation. Stop! If someone tells you that they love you and that they love God and they want to sleep with you before marriage, then by their actions they are demonstrating that they neither truly love you nor God. The Bible is clear on the following three things: if you love God, you'll do what he says; if you love others, you'll put them first and do what is right for them; and premarital sex is against God's will and causes havoc in hearts and lives. So if you love God, then you'll obey him, and if you love the one you're with, you'll want the best for them—that's why genuine love runs from premarital sex.

If you're married, the next step is to pray and give this area over to God. Find agreement with your spouse. Whenever the Bible shows God arranging a birth, he brings both parties in on the arrangement. Trying to have a child without the agreement of your spouse isn't right and will just lead to trouble. Couples should agree on these things before they even decide to get married.

No matter what your family picture currently looks like and regardless of where God leads you, take a chapter from Mary's life: embrace your situation and trust God to help you in it. When you feel tempted to complain or let your mind wander into the realm of "what about me and what I want," or even to think that it's too early or too late or too hard, remember Mary. She may be the most revered woman who ever lived, and it all started with two simple sentences: *"I am the Lord's servant. May it be to me as you have said."*

God loves you more than you can imagine, and he factors your desires and needs into the wisdom that he brings to your life. He wants the best possible future and eternity for both you and your children. TRUST HIM!

Practical Parenting TIPS *For Today*

Although it's best to follow God and trust him in everything, whether your child came according to your schedule or surprised you, you can rest assured she was no surprise to God. In the moment that she was conceived, God was there, creating her spirit and giving her a life and a future (Psalm 139). Take heart that God is faithful. He loves you and your child. He will make a way for you. The God who parted the Red Sea, who turned water into wine, can certainly turn a "surprise" into a blessing! Trust him!

CHAPTER 41

Joseph and Jesus:

Loving Someone Else's Kid

*M*ost Christmas stories focus on Mary and the baby Jesus. Yet the third character in the story also played an essential role in God's plan. Joseph remains a wonderful example to fathers today.

Joseph, a righteous, godly, Jewish man, would have been looking forward to getting married and having children in the traditional manner. Imagine how he must have felt when he learned of Mary's pregnancy! He certainly faced a huge dilemma, even if he believed Mary's story. If he took her home as his wife, he would be seen as admitting paternity and his reputation would be ruined. If he did not take her as his wife, Mary could have been, at best, made to live the rest of her life disgraced and unmarried, and at the worst, stoned to death.

Perhaps Joseph did believe Mary's story; maybe he heard confirmation from Mary's relative, Elizabeth, that this child was born of the Holy Spirit and was to be the Messiah. Some commentaries suggest it's possible that Joseph felt perplexed because he did believe, and wondered whether he was worthy to be the stepfather to the Messiah and husband to the Messiah's mother. Before all of this happened, marrying Mary was a simple fact of life; now it had become about Joseph's place in God's divine will and purpose.

In those days, if you were betrothed, it took a divorce to break off the engagement. Joseph chose an option that would cause the least grief. He decided to divorce her quietly without any public announcement.

Then the angel showed up and confirmed that the baby had come from the Holy Spirit. He told Joseph to have no fear about taking her home as his wife. Whether Joseph felt afraid because he believed or because he didn't, once he knew the truth and exactly what God wanted him to do, he obeyed without hesitation.

Joseph knew one thing for sure from then on—God had called him, Joseph, to be the earthly father of the Messiah. In ancient Jewish culture, adoption was absolute—once a child had been adopted, it became a moral and legal finality. A Jewish man looked forward to having his first son. The first son had a very important place in the religious and social life of the Jewish family, yet Joseph put aside all of his dreams and expectations about how his family would come together, and fully accepted Jesus as his firstborn son. Joseph accepted and treated God's Son as his own with no reservations. God's Word teaches us that because of Jesus' death, God accepts each one of us that is adopted into his family as completely his own—sons and daughters of God.

But when the time had fully come, God sent his Son, born of a woman, born under law, to redeem those under law, that we might receive the full rights of sons. Because you are sons, God sent the Spirit of his Son into our hearts, the Spirit who calls out, "Abba, Father." So you are no longer a slave, but a son; and since you are a son, God has made you also an heir." (Galatians 4:4–7)

Everyone adopted into God's family through Christ is treated as a birth child. The Bible says that we Christians are joint heirs with Christ. There are no second-class children in God's family, and even though Joseph had other sons, Jesus was his firstborn and he treated him fully as such.

Today, in this age of blended families, many of us have an excellent opportunity to model this kind of love and acceptance by treating all of those in our family—whether natural born, stepchildren, or adopted—with the same all-out love and care. God has no first- and second-class children, and neither should we.

Our natural minds fight with the idea that we can fully accept someone else's children and treat them the same as our own. Won't our own children somehow feel diminished? Certainly not! Our children know that they are ours and that we love them dearly, and showing that same love to others does not in any way take away from our genuine love for them. Loving everyone equally doesn't arouse sibling jealousy; favoritism does that. In fact, by demonstrating this kind of acceptance, we give all of the children in our household a wonderful foundation for understanding the awesome privilege of being adopted into God's family.

I watched a younger brother struggle with this issue before he married, and I felt proud of his struggle. My sister-in-law came to the relationship with two wonderful boys, and before making a final decision to marry her, my brother considered it long and hard. He struggled because he knew that he needed to accept and love those boys completely, as if they were his own, for the rest of his life. I felt proud of him because he didn't just make a marital decision based on his desires and view those boys as an afterthought. When he finally popped the question, he knew he was taking on a wife and two sons. Understand, the boys have a biological dad who sees them, and they don't even call my brother Dad—but they live with him and he loves them and treats them as if they were his own.

I find it interesting that God didn't send his angel to speak to Joseph right away. God gave Joseph time to consider the situation and weigh his options. Whatever he was struggling with, he more than likely considered the implications of becoming the father of this unexpected child. Joseph's obedience demonstrated that in his struggle he had already decided to do what was right, because when the angel told him what to do, he put his life and his desires on hold and accepted God's Son as his own.

God loves every child in your house and he wants you to do the right thing. Love them all as you would your own flesh and blood.

Practical Parenting
TIPS *For Today*

Raising children who are not your own, whether stepchildren or adopted children, requires significant prayer and intentional parenting. With biological children, you can often see the heredity shining through—and for good or bad, you likely know where certain traits and tendencies came from and how to deal with them. It is OK to admit that children who are not your biological children may be more difficult to understand. But that doesn't let you off the hook for treating *all* of the children in your household with equal love and dignity. The next time you have trouble relating to your step or adopted child, try looking at them as Joseph did—as an amazing gift from God, placed in your care.

CHAPTER 42

Mary & Joseph's Commitment:

Taking a Long-Term View of Marriage

When Joseph woke up, he did what the angel of the Lord had commanded him and took Mary home as his wife. (Matthew 1:24)

*W*hen Joseph heard God's will to him in regard to his upcoming marriage, he did *what the angel of the Lord had commanded him.*

God visited Mary after she was betrothed to Joseph but before they were married, and God's timing is always perfect.

He meant for Mary and Joseph to be man and wife and raise Jesus together, till death do they part, according to the way he created marriage to work.

Despite the gross inconveniences and interruptions to their lives, both Mary and Joseph stayed the course, not only because God gave them the task of parenting the Messiah, but because God commanded them to do so.

Earlier we talked about the two prophets who passed the baton of God's message from the Old Testament to the New, Malachi and John. They had a lot in common, including much of what they taught. They had one common teaching about which they both felt very passionate.

Both John and Malachi had a passion for "till death do us part" marriages. John's head ended up on a platter because he opposed Herod for marrying his brother's wife. And Malachi spent many verses rebuking those who left their marriage partners for others. I find really interesting God's reason for despising this idea, which Malachi clearly laid out:

> You ask, "Why?" It is because the Lord is acting as the witness between you and the wife of your youth, because you have broken faith with her, though she is your partner, the wife of your marriage covenant. Has not the Lord made them one? In flesh and spirit they are his. And why one? Because he was seeking godly offspring. So guard yourself in your spirit, and do not break faith with the wife of your youth.
>
> (Malachi 2:14–15, emphasis added)

In today's "me" culture, we often get duped into thinking

far too much about ourselves and the things that happen to us. Yet God calls us, as he did with Mary and Joseph, to focus even more on the part of his plan that goes beyond the span of our lives. Part of God's plan is for us to raise godly off-spring—not only because he loves them and wants to be with them forever, but also because in so doing, we get involved in strengthening and adding to the church and seeing that the gospel expands in the next generation.

In his first letter to the Corinthians, Paul admonished Christians to put their personal comfort in second place, in favor of advancing God's kingdom through their families:

> *For the unbelieving husband has been sanctified through his wife, and the unbelieving wife has been sanctified through her believing husband. Otherwise your children would be unclean, but as it is, they are holy.*
> (1 Corinthians 7:14)

Paul took Malachi's passionate words and called Christians in difficult marital situations to do what was right for the sake of their testimony and the effect it has on the next generation.

Jesus said that the Old Testament law allowed for divorce because of the hardness of the Israelites' hearts (Matthew 19:8). When we receive Christ as our savior, however, the Bible teaches that the Holy Spirit takes away our hearts of stone and replaces them with new, soft hearts, that with the help of the Holy Spirit can grow and learn and follow God in everything (Ezekiel 36:26–27).

It is God's will that we Christians be the salt and the light of the world, showing the unsaved by our lives what a relationship with and obedience to God looks like (Matthew 5:13–16). Jesus said that the world would be able to tell that we are his disciples through the love we show to each other (John 13:34–35). How can we demonstrate God's love if we can't even get our divorce rate below that of the people who aren't Christ's disciples? How can we show our children that God is love and that we are Christ's disciples when we're yelling and screaming at our spouse?

Perhaps God inspired both of these prophets to be so passionate about marriage vows because not doing so hampers our efforts at evangelism, both with our children and in the larger world. Our kids just don't understand how the faith we preach lines up with the nasty divorce they just experienced, while those in the world not only fail to see the love of God in operation in our marital unions, but see us as no different from them.

God wants us to allow the soft heart he put within us to take over. He wants us to learn to love and grow in love. And he wants to help us make our marriages work, not only for the sake of our own happiness, but also for the long-term view of furthering the kingdom of God.

Of course, we've all made mistakes. Thank God, he forgives and moves us forward. But if you find yourself contemplating a split with your souse, it's not too late to make a decision to do what is right. Go and get the help you need to make your marriage work. I would highly recommend the book, *Love and Respect: The Love She Most Desires, The Respect He Desperately Needs,* by Dr. Emerson Eggerichs. It's a powerful and practical book that will help you make your marriage work.

Mary and Joseph took a kingdom view of their marriage and obeyed God to stay together, work together, and raise a family together. Let's start today as a church and follow their excellent example.

Practical Parenting TIPS  *For Today*

Dr. Eggerichs' book explains why the Bible tells husbands to love their wives and why wives should respect their husbands. Men most need and desire respect, while women most crave love. Even if your marriage is in good shape, reading this book will help it get better. But no matter where your marriage is, I recommend you read it as a parent. Your son needs to learn what it means to love a woman and your daughter needs to learn how to respect a man. As well, once you recognize your son's blossoming need for respect and your daughter's need for love, you will be able to adapt your parenting for their individual needs.

CHAPTER 43

Jesus Presented in the Temple:

Child Dedication, Christening, and Confirmation

> On the eighth day, when it was time to circumcise him, he was named Jesus, the name the angel had given him before he had been conceived. When the time of their purification according to the Law of Moses had been completed, Joseph and Mary took him to Jerusalem to present him to the Lord (as it is written in the Law of the Lord, "Every firstborn male is to be consecrated to the Lord." (Luke 2:21–23)

*M*ary and Joseph followed the requirements of the Jewish law in regard to Jesus' birth. Eight days after Jesus was born in Bethlehem, he was circumcised and given his name.

The law required that every firstborn male be presented at the temple to be dedicated to the Lord, normally when a son reached thirty days of age. Mary also needed to present herself at the temple to offer a sacrifice for her postnatal purification when Jesus was forty days old. So Mary and Joseph either made the seven-mile journey from Bethlehem to Jerusalem and dedicated Jesus and then waited there for ten days, or they delayed the dedication (an acceptable practice) and did both on the same day, and then returned to live in Bethlehem before fleeing from Herod to Egypt. While in Jerusalem presenting Jesus at the temple, a righteous man named Simeon and a widow named Anna prayed for, spoke to, and prophesied over Jesus and Mary.

While no command in Scripture tells us to have a ceremony or dedication for our children today, by looking closely at this story, we can gain some insight into what we should focus on in regard to a religious ceremony for our children, if we choose to have one.

Mary and Joseph followed the Jewish law and the custom of their day and took Jesus through the requirements of both. As an infant, Jesus went through a circumcision ceremony. God does not require circumcision for Christians today, but we can still learn from the meaning behind the ceremony. Circumcision was to be performed on eight-day-old boys in order for them to be accepted into the community of Israel and benefit from the covenant with Abraham. It emphasized the obedience and commitment of the parents who followed God's instructions for their child. And it urged them to raise their child to know, serve, and follow God. Just because a man was circumcised as a child did not mean that he was automatically right with God for the rest of his life. When he grew older, he needed to take the circumcision into his heart and decide for himself to follow God. Without that, his circumcision became meaningless.

Next, Jesus went through the consecration of the firstborn son. God required this to remind the Israelites that he spared their firstborn when the angel of death brought the final plague on Egypt, killing all the Egyptians' firstborn. The first-born son was to be consecrated to God's service for his whole life. Since God gave the Levites that task, the parents could present their son at the temple, dedicate him to God's service, and then redeem him (buy him back) by paying five sanctu-ary shekels. The ceremony provides a wonderful picture of the parents recognizing God's sovereign will in the life of their children by dedicating the firstborn son to God and recogniz-ing that he belonged to God even before he was born.

Today, any ceremony should center on the same truths. Although the child is the focus, the ceremony should empha-size the parents' commitment to follow God in the raising of the child. No ceremony can secure an infant's eternal destiny. Each person must decide that for himself when he gets older.

A baby dedication ceremony also needs to offer the child into God's care, recognizing God's sovereign plan for the child and inviting God to be the Third Parent, working in both the child and the parents to fulfill his will for that child. To dedicate a child to God means to set them aside for God's purpose or plan. The underlying intent of the word *dedication* denotes initiation. Once the temple and its contents were completed, the people dedicated the holy things to God for use in his service. A Hebrew word translated "dedicate" in the Old Testament, *hanak*, is the term used in this very well known verse:

> *Train a child in the way he should go, and when he is old he will not turn from it.* (Proverbs 22:6)

The verse means "to dedicate a child" or to start them off following God and serving him, and when they are old they will not turn from it. The dedication is only the starting point. It must be followed up with a day-to-day dedication, which involves bringing your children up God's way.

Jesus' dedication also took place in the temple, attended by righteous witnesses waiting for Jesus' birth. Simeon and Anna did not know Mary and Joseph, or Jesus, but they had been expecting the Messiah, and through the Spirit recognized the baby as the coming One.

When we dedicate our children to God, we are dedicating them through Christ, raising them to become part of the church of the firstborn: *"To the church of the firstborn, whose names are written in heaven"* (Hebrews 12:23). Whether they are male or female, or first- or tenth-born, we stand in the church as Mary and Joseph stood in the temple and dedicate our children to follow God's firstborn Son, Jesus.

The Bible says that Jesus is God's firstborn and that we, as Christians, are joint heirs with him. Not joint heirs as in, we'll inherit alongside him like a second- or third-born, but joint in the position of firstborn. We didn't get into the kingdom after Jesus, but because of him. We enter through Christ, because of what he did—and God sees us as he sees Jesus. In God's eyes, we are all firstborn.

All of this to say, child dedication ceremonies are a great idea that follows a great Judeo-Christian heritage of publicly committing parents, children, and witnesses to establishing God's truth in a child's life. Regardless of the ceremony and elements used, if you focus on the purposes and truths just established, you'll be blessed in many ways.

Just like Mary and Joseph, follow through on your commitment to raise your child God's way and with his help. A child dedication without follow-through is like having a wedding just for the sake of the celebration, and then not saying, "I do."

So make it a celebration! We don't have many greater reasons to celebrate than over the anticipation of our children growing up and living in God's will.

Practical Parenting
TIPS *For Today*

A public dedication ceremony should be attended by family, friends, and fellow church-goers, all of whom can witness your commitment to God to raise the child right. In turn, they should commit to help you and your child follow God. If the tradition in your church will accept it, invite one or more family members or friends who walk closely with God to be involved in the ceremony, to speak a personal blessing or admonition, or say a prayer for your family. Ask these special people to write a message of spiritual encouragement to your child. And take lots of pictures. Sharing this time with your child when he or she gets older is a powerful way to show them that their life was rooted and grounded in God from the start.

CHAPTER 44

Jesus the Tween:

Encouraging
Spiritual Growth

*T*he Bible gives us only one brief glimpse into Jesus' boy-hood, but even this quick story provides parents a wealth of help (Luke 2:41–52).

At the age of twelve, Jesus traveled with his family and a caravan of friends and relatives to Jerusalem to celebrate the Passover. Jewish men were required to go to the temple three times a year for feast days; those who lived a long ways away would make the journey at least once a year for the Passover, the greatest of the three feasts. Nazareth was more than seventy miles from Jerusalem, so even if Joseph went down three times a year, he may have gone alone the other two times. On this occasion he, Mary, and Jesus traveled together.

When the feast ended, everyone, except Jesus, packed up and headed back to Nazareth. It took a day of travel for Mary and Joseph to realize that Jesus wasn't around. Why didn't they notice his absence earlier? They were traveling in a large group and the women and children would have traveled together in the caravan separate from the men. Jesus, at twelve, was right at the age where he would have been able to travel in either group. It's likely that Joseph thought Jesus was with Mary, while Mary thought he was with Joseph.

By the time Mary and Joseph located Jesus in the temple, he had been there for three days. Upon their arrival they found him sitting with the teachers and amazing them with his understanding and answers (Luke 2:46–47).

If you don't think about this passage in light of others, you could pass over this event thinking, *Of course he blew the teachers away; he was God's Son.* We need to remember that Jesus temporarily laid aside his heavenly glory as God's Son and became like one of us so that we could identify with him and follow his example. He had to learn and grow up, just like every other child. He therefore provides an example for our children and lets them know that when they pray about their struggles, Jesus understands.

Jesus did have one thing over every child ever born on the planet: he arrived without sin. As the son of a virgin, he lacked the original sin that separates every child from God, from Cain onward. Jesus grew up in fellowship with God, enjoying his love and help from day one.

So how can our children, born with original sin, identify with Jesus? They accept Jesus' death on the cross, repent of their sins, and ask God into their heart and commit to follow his ways and live for him. God then wipes away their sin and adopts them as his own. From that point forward, they can grow up in God's special presence with his love, guidance, wisdom, correction, and help, just as Jesus did.

Further, they have God's Spirit ready to help them learn and understand. We should not underestimate our children's ability to grow in Christ, but embrace Jesus' example and encourage them to grow as he did. And how can we best facilitate this spiritual development?

We all understand that in order to teach math, or anything else for that matter, the teaching must be intentional, consistent, and progressive. Every school has a math curriculum; it's taught every year, and each grade's lessons lay the foundation for the following year. Nothing is taught haphazardly or left to chance. Yet when it comes to a spiritual education, the effort is often very "hit or miss."

Kids can't learn spiritual training by osmosis; they need to be taught. Therefore we need to get proactive and creative and preside over our children's spiritual growth. I suggest that each parent think and pray through, and then write and carry out a purposeful and progressive plan.

Allow me to give you some guidelines and suggestions for how to develop an easy and effective plan to help you accelerate your child's spiritual growth. If your spouse has agreed to partner-parenting, then suggest that you break out the pen and notepad and go over these suggestions and develop a plan together.

First, let's establish what is necessary for spiritual growth. If you study the New Testament letters, you'll find that Paul, Peter, and John all encourage Christians to grow and move toward maturity in their faith. They instruct us to grow in three primary categories: knowledge of our faith; our personal relationship with God; and the daily living out of our faith.

The word *Christian* means to be Christlike, and Jesus lived a life in close fellowship with God. He knew and understood God's Word, and he lived out what he knew and believed.

Christian children must grow and mature in the same way, with all three legs of the Christian growth stool. Knowing this, it's easy to understand why God has appointed parents to oversee their children's spiritual growth. You can get help from the church, especially to help your children grow in the knowledge of their faith. The other two legs of the stool—growth in their relationship with God and living out their faith—must happen in the context of daily life, and therefore cannot be overseen by the church. It is impossible to facilitate a child's spiritual growth merely by taking them to church a few hours a week.

Jesus learned the Torah in school; he attended the synagogue and attended the feasts at the Jerusalem temple; but the biggest part of his spiritual training took place in his home. Mary and Joseph's track record clearly demonstrates that they followed God's instructions.

Let's now look at some practical ways to facilitate your child's progress in each of the three areas of spiritual growth.

1. *Growing in the knowledge of their faith.* Attending a church with a strong children's program that teaches God's Word is a good foundation. You cannot rely on this alone, though, because your child needs to know a lot more than what he or she can learn in church.

I suggest you meet briefly with the person in charge of selecting the children's curriculum and find out what the church is teaching your children. You might want to find out, as well, if they change curriculums more than once a year so that you can stay current. Once you know, go to the local Christian bookstore (or Internet if you don't have a Christian bookstore near you) and find a book or two for children that will help reinforce what the church teaches.

Also, find other age-appropriate materials that will help your children at home. Several good Christian videos, tapes, and books can help you get the task done. Be careful when choosing these items, though, to check that you're teaching your children in different areas. The objective of some Christian video series, for example, is to teach life lessons, while others feature animated Bible stories that help familiarize your child with the Bible. It would be good to use both, as opposed to getting more than one series that teaches only life lessons.

Make a habit of talking to your children about what they learn in church and also about what you're currently learning or how a current event should be viewed biblically. Show them how faith is weaved throughout your daily life.

Finally, help your children develop the habit of daily Bible reading. Buy an age-appropriate Bible storybook or Bible and help them chart a reading program, and then stay with it.

2. *Growing in their relationship with God.* Helping your child develop their own personal, daily quiet time or devotional time with God is probably one of the most important things you can do to help your child grow in their relationship with God. For tips on this, turn to chapter 24 of this book (*"The Samuel Stages: Spiritual Growth One Stage at a Time"*).

3. *Growing in the daily living out of their faith.* Being a Christian isn't only about believing the right things; it's about being and acting Christ like—learning to love others with our thoughts, words, and deeds. Ask God to help you get into the habit of teaching your children from the Bible in the heat of the moment and in the middle of everyday life. When the last cookie gets grabbed and the squabble is on, use God's Word to teach them how to do it better and why God says that's important.

The story of Jesus' boyhood trip to the temple ends with a very inspirational verse:

> *And Jesus grew in wisdom and stature, and in favor with God and men.* (Luke 2:52)

Some live their life as if Christianity were like a side order of fries to put down alongside their hamburger of life; it's not. Christianity is the plate, the foundation, for who we are and how we think, speak, and behave. Before sin entered the scene, Adam and Eve didn't have a religion; they had a loving creator who made everything for them and wanted to teach them how life worked and help them learn and grow, be blessed, and cover the earth.

Helping our children grow spiritually isn't about making them mini-religious fanatics, but about introducing them to a loving heavenly Father who wants to help them learn how he made all of life to work, both now and for eternity.

Practical Parenting
TIPS

For Today

To build your child's spiritual knowledge, the following list suggests some excellent resources you might consider:
801 Questions Children Ask about God and the Bible.
Teaching Your Child How to Pray
Teaching Your Child about God
The Singing Bible
The Memory Bible
Spiritual Training of Children
100 Bible Stories 100 Bible Songs
God's Great News for Children

CHAPTER 45

A Trip to the Temple, Part 1:

The Importance of Careful Discipline

The only commandment the Bible directs specifically toward children requires that they honor and obey their parents. This should provide a large clue about the importance of this command—important not only for the children to learn but also essential for parents to understand, teach, and enforce.

The brief story of the boy Jesus staying at the temple when his parents left Jerusalem, thinking he was with them, gives us some insight into this key parenting issue. It takes discipline to make sure your children obey. In this first of a two-part look at Jesus at the temple, we'll see the importance of remaining thoughtful in what we require and that we apply discipline carefully.

When Mary and Joseph finally found Jesus three days after they lost track of him, an interesting drama played out:

> *When his parents saw him, they were astonished. His mother said to him, "Son, why have you treated us like this? Your father and I have been anxiously searching for you." "Why were you searching for me?" he asked. "Didn't you know I had to be in my Father's house?" But they did not understand what he was saying to them.* (Luke 2:48–50)

Try to imagine what Mary must have been going through. Remember that she and Joseph had departed to Egypt immediately after Jesus' birth to prevent Herod from killing the baby. No doubt they later learned of all the children Herod had murdered. They knew Jesus was the Messiah and that if evil men like Herod figured out his identity, he'd be in trouble. So when the twelve-year-old Jesus went missing, Mary and Joseph felt understandably scared. Here God had entrusted them with caring for the Messiah, and they had lost him in the city where Herod's son ruled.

At first glance, Jesus' disappearance seems a bit dishonoring to his parents, and perhaps even disobedient. As parents, our initial reaction when our kids dishonor, disrespect, or disobey sets the tone for how we solve the problem. But, note that before Mary reacted, she explained her concern and allowed Jesus to explain the reason for his behavior.

Mary essentially asked Jesus why he had done something that she considered either wrong, dishonoring, or at very least, inconsiderate. Jesus let his mother know that he had assumed his parents would know where he was and that they would approve of it. Jesus and his parents had their wires crossed, but he never meant to disrespect or disobey them.

It appears from Mary's comments that she thought Jesus should have known better; but she checked to make sure. When it comes to disciplining your children, it's very important that you, like Mary, explain how things look from your vantage point and then ask questions before doling out rebukes or punishments.

> *His mother said to him, "Son, why have you treated us like this? Your father and I have been anxiously searching for you."* (Luke 2:48b)

Regain a cool head if you need to and check to see if your child needs correction, or simply did not understand and needs training. Punishing children when they need training can frustrate or discourage them and hinder progress: *"Fathers, do not embitter your children, or they will become discouraged"* (Colossians 3:21).

Through Moses, God promised that children would live long and do well if they honored their parents. In context, Moses first taught the adults that they must honor and obey God. So, the parents were admonished to honor and obey God, and the children were told to honor and obey their parents.

Paul repeated and updated the fifth commandment teaching in a New Testament context:

> *Children, obey your parents in the Lord, for this is right. "Honor your father and mother"—which is the first commandment with a promise—"that it may go well with you and that you may enjoy long life on the earth."* (Ephesians 6:13, emphasis added)

Paul changed the word *land* (Promised Land) to *earth*, expanding the commandment and its blessing to include Christians of every nation. He clarifies the context of the commandment by adding, "Children, obey your parents **in the Lord**" (emphasis added).

God requires our children to honor and obey us so that we can teach them how to honor and obey God. God loves your children and wants them to follow him and be blessed. He loves you and wants you to be blessed in that process; but if you don't obey and follow God yourself and then teach your children to do the same, you're going to have a tough time getting your children to honor and obey you.

The flipside is that God promises to bless your children if you teach them to follow him, and if they obey and listen to you. When you do things his way, he will back you up and help you.

Realizing the context of children being required to obey and honor you helps you to get the job done. If the issue is really about your children following God, you will be a little more careful about what you require and how you respond. Mary was evidently a little upset about how she perceived that she and Joseph had been treated; but she slowed down and investigated, to make sure. Sometimes we let our personal feelings get in the way when we feel that we've been disrespected or disobeyed. Remembering that it's more about our child's relationship with God and being obedient to him will help us get our mind off of ourselves and onto how God views the situation.

Remembering the context of the commandment also helps us remember that our children are not our personal slaves;

God requires them to obey us so that we can direct them toward him and his commands.

Finally, if it really is about obeying God, then we need to remember that any discipline we hand out should reflect God's loving discipline and should never be motivated out of our hurt or anger.

Consider a few tips gleaned from Mary and Joseph's example:

1. *Mary and Joseph knew and would have taught God's fifth commandment promise to Jesus.*

God demonstrates his own approach to children in the fifth commandment: if you honor your parents, you get rewarded. Bribing a child is using a reward to convince the child to do what the parent wants—that is not God's approach. He asks for honor and respect and, once he has it, he rewards it. Follow God's lead and thank and praise your children for cooperating with you. Give them a hug and tell them how wonderful you think they are; and when they're extra helpful, find extra special ways to reward them. Rewarding your child's respect and obedience sends a powerful message that doing things the right way brings good into their lives. A child who consistently sees the rewards of their actions will think twice before putting those rewards in jeopardy.

2. *Mary acknowledged that in parenting, she was God's servant.*

Jesus taught that those in authority must serve the ones he leads. The fact that God has required your children to honor you means he requires that you serve them, not vice versa. Be careful to never selfishly misuse your authority over your children. Everything God asks us to do will ultimately benefit us; we should have the same objective in mind every time we tell our children to do or not do something. Everyone, including children, finds it easier to obey someone who consistently shows that they have their best interests in mind.

Gaining your child's eager cooperation is better than trying to push them. Ask nicely and say please; use commands and demands only as a last resort. We all find it easier to cooperate, honor, or obey when we get asked rather than when we're commanded.

3. *Mary and Joseph allowed Jesus to ask questions when confronted.*

Mary and Joseph stated their grievance to the twelve-year-old Jesus and then asked a question to allow him the opportunity to explain himself. The boy Jesus didn't understand his parents' anxiety and the implication that he'd done something wrong or inconsiderate, so he asked them two questions.

Asking questions is the most appropriate form of conversation when a situation has gone south, because the answers to those questions help both parties understand each other's vantage point and stop anyone from jumping to invalid conclusions. Allow your children to ask you reasonable questions when they are asked or told to do something. When they do, listen carefully and answer them calmly. If they have a compromise or a valid objection, factor it in and reconsider. This is very beneficial on many levels. It demonstrates to your children that obedience is truly cooperative and beneficial to all; it prevents them from feeling that they are merely slaves sent on lowly errands; and it prepares them for life by teaching them intelligent obedience instead of blind obedience.

Jesus grew up to be a cooperative, obedient member of his society, but he was never blindly obedient. He spoke out when the religious leaders enforced extra-biblical laws that tended to line their pockets. He politely reminded Pilate that God was in charge, not the governor; and he questioned the temple guard who struck him unjustly. Children allowed to respectfully question authority will better understand how it works and how it benefits them, and therefore will learn to cooperate with the system.

4. *Mary and Joseph did not start by threatening or punishing Jesus; they got the facts and moved forward.*

When your child acts in dishonoring ways, helping him understand and obey the next time is the goal. When your children disobey, it's best to not automatically head in the direction of punishment; the goal is to train them and help them understand and obey. Punishment is not always the best way to achieve that objective.

Go through the questioning stage so that any misunderstandings can be discovered. If the transgression comes down to direct disobedience and it's a first offense, then a calm, private, boundary-drawing conversation is in order. Talk it out and explain again the purpose and benefits of cooperation and obedience in the family and in life. Address their specific act of disrespect or disobedience and cover specifically and practically how it will negatively impact their life. Also cover why an alternate choice would have been more beneficial.

If it's not the first offense but you've never had this kind of calm, reasoning conversation with them, then you may want to try it and give them another chance. A child who's shown mercy and given another chance will often respond better than if he had been punished.

When we apply ourselves to this foundation, God's fifth commandment promise begins to bless our home. Family relationships start to go well, and family life becomes more enjoyable. *"That it may go well with you and that you may enjoy long life on the earth."*

Mary, Joseph, and Jesus are our example, and they showed us that it can be done.

Practical Parenting **TIPS** *For Today*

If your child has disobeyed or disrespected you, try this before you dole out a punishment. Ask questions and bring your child into the conversation to explain the reason why he acted as he did. Listen attentively whenever he talks. At the end of the conversation, assess whether they've grasped your point and will refrain from repeating the behavior; if so, then perhaps punishment is not necessary, since you've already reached your objective. Praise them for listening, learning, and making the right choice, and let them know with a hug to, basically, "go and sin no more."

CHAPTER 46

A Trip to the Temple, Part 2:

The Importance God Places on Honor and Obedience

> *Children, obey [honor] your parents in the Lord for this is right.*
> (Ephesians 6:1, parenthetical word added)

The story of the boy Jesus at the temple shows us that it's our job to teach our children the importance of honoring and obeying authorities. It also suggests how we can do that.

The word *honor* originally comes from a Hebrew word that means *to be heavy*. It implies "to give weight to" or give honor, credit, and respect to. In the Bible the primary way a person shows honor to God or to other authorities is through their obedience—in other words, the proof of honor is obedience. For children, the first lesson in honoring their parents is to obey them.

Remember that Jesus stayed at the temple, conversing with religious authorities, after his parents left Jerusalem in the mistaken notion that he was among their caravan heading home. Mary and Joseph felt understandably anxious when they found their twelve-year-old, Jesus, three days after they lost track of him.

> *When his parents saw him, they were astonished. His mother said to him, "Son, why have you treated us like this? Your father and I have been anxiously searching for you." "Why were you searching for me?" he asked. "Didn't you know I had to be in my Father's house?" But they did not understand what he was saying to them.*
> (Luke 2:48–50)

After Mary and Joseph and Jesus had their family conference in the temple, we see a quick and clear outcome to the proceedings. Whether Mary and Joseph had felt that Jesus had disobeyed or dishonored them, Luke tells us that they took care of the situation so that it would not happen again. And Jesus cooperated: *"Then he went down to Nazareth with them and was obedient to them"* (Luke 2:51).

Obedience is lesson number one for children, for two reasons. The most obvious, of course, is that if a child doesn't obey and understand the function and importance of obedience, then you can't teach him a thing—because he isn't listening. Second, obedience is the first principle of all cooperative social structures, and a child who never learns to submit to authority will never be able to function effectively in life.

Often, when a child disobeys, the problem isn't that he has chosen to willfully rebel, but that he has never been taught the purpose, principles, and practice of obedience.

As parents, it's our job to teach obedience and help our children understand it and its benefits. Next we are to train them, step by step, how to walk in it. Only then do we discipline them to ensure that they comply.

Consider these practical parenting tips, suggested by Mary and Joseph, concerning teaching our children about obedience:

1. *Jesus was taught and understood the importance of authority and obedience.*

Explain to your children that obedience will help them enjoy a good life. God promised that he would bless them if they obey both you and him. Part of that blessing is a very practical thing. Obedience isn't about being the low guy on the totem pole; it's about having a system for cooperating in a home, society, and country, so that things work smoothly.

Children should obey their parents because it makes it easier for the parents to teach their child and prepare them for leading a good life. At work, everyone obeys the boss in order to help the company run better and do well, so that everyone can keep their jobs. In society, we obey laws designed to protect us and help us all live together happily. Everyone needs to obey God so that he can love us and help us.

Tell your children that it's very important to learn the life-skill of obedience because it's required all through life and will help them do well. Use Jesus at age twelve as an example—he's God, he created the world, but when he lived here, he obeyed because he knew that obedience is a blessing that helps make our lives better.

Reinforce this lesson every time you need to remind your children to obey. Many children who end up disobeying misunderstand obedience as something negative. They think that as soon as they're adults, they'll be able to throw off the nasty shackles of obedience and do whatever they want. If you have older kids who already think like this, let them know it's not true.

2. Mary and Joseph didn't berate Jesus' person or character; they taught him and encouraged him forward.

Follow God's lead in how you address your children. When we become Christians, God gives us the righteousness of Christ because of what Jesus did for us. From that point forward, God sees us as righteous and helps us grow into his vision for us (Romans 3:22; Philippians 1:8–11). When our children become Christians, the same is true for them; and as their parents, we need to get in step with God by seeing them the way he sees them.

When you make a mistake or blow it big time, God doesn't take away his gift of righteousness and call you names. He still sees you as righteous and continues to help you toward that goal. He forgives you, helps you up, and encourages you to move toward the target. When our children dishonor us in words or actions, when they make mistakes or blow it, we need to do for them what God does for us by believing in them and the power of God working in them, encouraging them in their righteousness and forward motion.

When we berate our children by calling them "bad," "stupid," or other names, we cause them to identify with their sin nature instead of God's gift and his goal for them. When your children do something bad, it doesn't mean that they are bad; only that they did something bad.

Let the words you say to your children, even in correction, always confirm that they're righteous and still heading in the right direction—good kids growing and learning to become even more wonderful. A person who sees herself as obedient will, for the most part, act accordingly.

3. *Mary and Joseph led by example, obeying God and the other authorities over them.*

If your children see you calling in to work sick when you're not, cheating on your income taxes, and going out the back door at church when everyone has been asked not to use that door, all of your teaching and explanations will count for nothing. Even the old-fashioned (wrong) way of trying to make them obey—with all of its yelling, scolding, threatening, and punishments—will ultimately fail.

Remember that obedience is merely the core of honor. Here's an easy but complete definition for honor that children understand: listen, respect, and obey.

Only the fifth commandment is directed at children. On the surface, it may appear to be designed to make our lives easier. In fact, with the command, God is showing us how important and essential it is for us to train our children in obedience.

Practical Parenting TIPS For Today

Be sure that you teach your children that blind obedience is never required. They are always allowed to politely and respectfully explain themselves and ask questions if they don't understand. Also, God requires children to obey parents and those with whom the parents choose to share that authority, but God gave that authority to help parents train their children to follow God. Let your children know that God does not require them to obey any authority figure who tells them to do something wrong.

CHAPTER 47

Mary's Treasure:

Watching Your Children with an Ear to God

*M*any years ago I temporarily filled the shoes of associate pastor. During those two to three years, I felt amazed by a certain gifting that comes with God putting you in that office. Each week I prayed for, counseled, taught, and helped different members of the church. As I struggled to serve effectively and prayed for help, God gave me not only a heart for the people, but insight into the true identity of each of them and what God was trying to do in their lives.

I recalled this recently while talking to a pastor about his Sunday morning responsibilities. He said that although preaching and teaching on Sunday morning was work, he considered it the easiest of his responsibilities. Memories of how I felt walking into the church where I pastored years earlier flooded back to me. A pastor walks into the assembly and starts looking at each face, getting updates, praying silently, receiving God's insights, caring, loving, and trying his best to maintain hope for each person and encourage each person forward. It's a wonderful gift.

Has one of your pastors or leaders ever just looked at you and known that something was amiss? I have experienced it, and I marvel at the sense of God's overwhelming love that comes with it.

I've seen this same gifting in operation whenever God has given me a task that involves caring for others. When God wants you to care for someone, he will give you the love, grace, insight, and wisdom that you need to do the job well. The Bible is full of examples of God working through those he's called to be in authority. He gave wisdom to David and gave him insight into the hearts of the men who labored in his court. Moses knew the hearts of the Israelites and was given wisdom to lead them. Joseph received divine insight into the lives of those he looked after in prison. Jesus was often given insight into his disciples' thoughts or discussions. Paul demonstrated the insight God gave him into the needs of each congregation through the letters he wrote to them.

Parenting is a God-given role of authority and, as with other tasks of authority, God gives insight and wisdom to parents who look to him for help. I believe that Mary modeled the key to operating this parenting gift.

In order to receive insight and wisdom for the ones you serve, several factors must be in place. First, you must have the heart of a servant and truly care for, love, and want the best for those you lead. This puts you in tune with God's heart. Next, you have to look to God for his help and trust him to guide and help you as you go. Third, you must watch and consider. If you truly love those you lead, then you'll observe them, think about what you see, and ponder and pray about what needs to be done. Often, when you care for people and observe them, you'll remember and note things they said and did or the things others said about them; then some time later, God will bring several of the things you observed together, show you a pattern, and help you speak positively into their lives.

We know that Mary and Joseph loved Jesus, and we see them relying on God's assistance and help at every turn of the story. Mary watched and pondered everything that happened concerning Jesus.

> *But Mary treasured [remembered] up all these things and pondered [thought deeply about] them in her heart.* (Luke 2:19, parenthetical comments added)

> *Then he went down to Nazareth with them and was obedient to them. But his mother treasured [remembered and considered deeply] all these things in her heart.* (Luke 2:51, parenthetical comments added)

When something happened in Jesus' life, Mary took note; she filed it away and churned it over in her mind. Mary had all three leadership "insight" tools in place.

Ask God to give you the insight and wisdom you need to help you actively watch and listen to your children and what happens around them, and to notice and remember things that might help later.

We tend to do this naturally. We get to know our children and their habits well enough that often we know what they are doing without looking, and how they're going to respond before they do. That's commonly referred to as "mothers having eyes in the back of their heads." That's a good thing—but what I'm talking about goes a big step beyond that and brings God into the loop.

Mary remembered and pondered the story the shepherds told. She meditated on the comments of the twelve-year-old Jesus at the temple. She had to consider these things prayerfully because they were about what God was doing—and going to do—in Jesus' life. Mary watched Jesus with her ear tuned to God.

We don't understand everything that's going on in our child's heart and life, but God does. At the time, Mary felt content with not understanding everything the shepherds declared and not comprehending what Jesus said at the temple. She knew they were important, so she watched, listened, and pondered the events, saving the information and her possible conclusions until God could use them to assist her in her task.

The next time your child does or says something that stands out for some reason (good or bad), don't leap to a conclusion—turn your ear to God and ponder prayerfully. God could show you what led to the misunderstanding or the origin of the wrong idea lodged in your child's mind. He could also show you something about their personality or unique gifting that may help you in directing them in the future. Or he may even use what you see or hear to show you something about your parenting to encourage or help you in your task.

A friend of mine was having a very difficult time with his young son. It seemed that no matter what he did to encourage his boy to be kind, caring, and good, it just didn't "take." His son had only recently started to misbehave and disobey, and much to this father's dismay, the boy seemed to be identifying himself with being bad instead of good.

A few days after my friend began praying intently about
this, looking for a solution, he was working in a room next
to where his two sons were playing with their action figures.
His thoughts continually wandered away from his work and
toward his sons. Finally, sensing that he needed to listen,
he put down his work and tuned into his sons. The son he
was having trouble with had taken the role of the bad guy
and was doing a great job at it. Suddenly the pieces came
together—the older son always insisted on being the good
guy, which left his second son always the bad guy. He knew
right away that the imaginative "bad guy" role-playing was
molding his son.

When my friend talked with his son and dealt with the
unbalanced play, he saw an immediate and drastic change.
Only by loving his son, praying for God's help, and then
watching, listening, and pondering, did he unlock the
problem.

What Mary locked in her heart during Jesus' early years
even helped her when he got older. The Gospel writers record
that Jesus' mother and brothers objected to how Jesus ran his
public ministry (Mark 3:20–21, 31–35; John 7:1–9). Years
later, after Mary became a Christian, she was among the
believers in the upper room on Pentecost when the Holy
Spirit came. The things that Mary had remembered and pondered all pointed to Jesus being God's Son and the Savior of
the world. It seems that God helped Mary put the needle of
her pondering through the correct points along the fabric of
her treasured thoughts, and finally bring them all together.

In a similar way, ask God to help you use this wonderful
gift to help you raise his children.

Practical Parenting TIPS  *For Today*

Hindsight is 20/20. Sometimes blow-ups, anger, and moodiness appear to be singular instances, when in fact they may form a pattern. For example, your daughter may act excessively grumpy the week before her period. Or your four-year-old may become a terror around five o'clock every afternoon—about the time her blood sugar crashes. Make mental notes to remember, journal, or even jot down observations on a calendar to help you see any possible association between them and the times these undesirable actions occur. It may be as simple as giving a four-year-old a light snack at 4:45 p.m. every day!

CHAPTER 48

Mary, Joseph, Jesus, and the Synagogue:

The Importance of Church

*He went to Nazareth, where **he had been brought up**, and on the Sabbath day he went into the synagogue, **as was his custom**. And he stood up to read.*
(Luke 4:16, emphasis added)

*M*ary and Joseph followed the Jewish law and the customs of their day in regard to temple worship and synagogue attendance. They taught Jesus to do the same. They took him to the temple for his dedication and made the seventy-plus-mile journey from Nazareth to attend the required annual feast day celebrations. Jesus would have received his formal education at the synagogue, and as we see from the verse above, as an adult he attended Sabbath services every week.

If anyone ever had the right to skip weekly services because the place reeked of hypocrites, it was Jesus. He was the first to use the word *hypocrite* in the way we understand it today— in Jesus day, the word referred to stage actors. Mary and Joseph raised Jesus' to attend and love God's places of worship, and he attended despite the hypocrites.

Mary and Joseph knew from the Old Testament the crucial importance of attending the special feast days and regular services, and how essential it was for them to get help teaching Jesus the Scriptures. And by their example, they have passed the torch to us.

The social, cultural, and spiritual context is different for us today than it was for Joseph's family, but the core purposes and benefits for attending regular services and the requirement to attend has not changed at all.

The writer of the Book of Hebrews wrote:

> *And let us consider how we may spur one another on toward love and good deeds. Let us not give up meeting together, as some are in the habit of doing, but let us encourage one another—and all the more as you see the Day approaching.* (Hebrews 10:24–25)

This is the only New Testament verse that expressly tells Christians to meet together regularly, which has caused some to believe that it must be of little importance. Nothing could be further from the truth. Actually, the New Testament writers felt that regular corporate worship was so obvious that it didn't need to be repeatedly commanded.

Jesus, our example, made a habit of always attending the temple and the synagogue and getting involved there. The Book of Acts describes how the disciples, under the direction of the Holy Spirit, spread the gospel and started churches where Christians could meet. Paul continued to attend synagogue after his conversion for the purpose of spreading the Good News, and he set up churches in cities all over the world. The New Testament is largely made up of letters from church leaders to churches. Those letters talk about appointing deacons, elders, and other church leaders; how a church service should run; how each Christian can use their gifts to serve the church; church finance; church unity; church planting; various ministries within the church; church sacraments; worship and orderly services; the disciplining of church leaders; the expulsion of unrepentant sinners from the church; and church growth. The letters even address favoritism in the way we seat people in church.

The last book of the Bible begins with letters to seven New Testament era churches and lets us know that Jesus is returning for his church. In order to logically conclude that church and church attendance is not God's idea—in fact, it is a very important part of his plan—a person would have to ignore the entire history and context of the New Testament.

We—that is, Christians—are the church, not the building where the church meets. The New Testament calls us the church in the context of our meeting together.

As one preacher said, sitting in church doesn't make you a Christian any more than sitting in a garage makes you a car. Some have used this cute saying to espouse the idea that you don't have to go to church to be a Christian. True enough. But if you're a Christian, you are part of the church and God wants you to attend and get involved in a local chapter.

As parents, we need to know that God set up this system to facilitate the spiritual growth and encouragement of his children and the spread of the gospel. If we want to raise our children God's way and see their lives blessed by God, then we need to follow Mary and Joseph's lead and plug our children regularly and effectively into God's plan for the local church.

Here are some FAQs about kids and church that'll help you get the most out of plugging your children in:

1. *Are there right and wrong churches to attend?*

Mary and Joseph attended where God's Word was taught.

Of course, the choice for Jesus' parents was a little more straightforward than it can be for us today. Nevertheless, we can learn from what they did. They attended the temple on special days, and the synagogue regularly, to obey God, to learn God's Word, and to fellowship with other believers in a community designed to strengthen and encourage each others faith and growth.

We need to focus on the core of these purposes. Does the church in question believe that the Bible is God's inspired Word? Does it teach the Word so that listeners can apply it to their lives?

There are really only three types of churches: those that pervert the truth; those that water down the truth; and those that teach the truth. Stay away from the first category; these churches don't believe in the basic tenets of the Christian faith. Churches in this category may deny that Jesus is God, or that God is one Lord made up of three persons, or that accepting Jesus' sacrifice is the only way to God. These churches will often claim to be the only ones with the truth, or claim that everyone has their own truth, and put more emphasis on being a part of their church than they do on building a personal relationship with God through Christ.

Churches that water down the truth may be new churches so focused on outreach that they teach what people want to hear, or they may be established churches who have been members of long-time Christian denominations that in recent decades have fallen away from believing that the Bible is God's infallible Word (2 Timothy 3:16). If their doctrine and church policy are changing and being updated to reflect society's current ideas of right and wrong, with no regard for what the Bible says, then run, don't walk, to the nearest exit.

Many churches fall into the third category. They all have slightly different emphases in their doctrine, varying approaches in their worship, and they may disagree on issues not central to the faith—but they all agree on the basic tenets of the Christian faith. Even though they may not always see eye to eye, they will readily accept other churches in this category as legitimate Christian churches. These churches believe in God's Word and its power to change lives, and preach it for life application (Ephesians 4:5).

If the Bible's teaching compels us to take our family to church and shows us that the purpose for going is to learn the Bible and apply it to our lives and be supported by our fellow worshipers, then we need to attend a place that believes and teaches the Bible. Anything else would be a contradiction in logic.

2. How do I decide on which church to attend?

Mary and Joseph attended services in their local community.

If after considering the information above you still have several churches to choose from, consider a few personal objectives to help you decide.

Community: Mary and Joseph attended the synagogue in their community and traveled with their friends and family to the temple in Jerusalem. Mary and Joseph lived among the people with whom they attended church. It's hard to be supported in your spiritual growth by people who don't know you and who see you only once a week.

If you have the option of attending a Bible-believing Christian church where you, your spouse, and your children already know people, then that's probably the right place. Remember, this won't always be the closest church. Travel has become much easier since Jesus' day, and therefore community doesn't have to be made up of the people who live in your immediate neighborhood. Your community is better defined by the people who know you and spend time with you.

Programs for your children: Mary and Joseph would have had help from the synagogue in teaching the Bible to Jesus. Although it's our job to disciple our children at home, church can and should lend support. When choosing a church, find out what the children's department and youth group are doing to assist you in teaching your children God's Word. Community is an important aspect of church for your child, so some fun and good times should be built into their church programs—but if it's all about fun and games with a sprinkle of Bible, you'll probably get more effective assistance from another church.

Personal preference: If you've considered all the above and still have a few options open, then your personal preference can come into play. If you were raised in a certain church and feel comfortable with that style of worship, or if you just feel more at home in a certain church, then choose it. But resist the temptation to put personal preference and comfort over more important considerations. If God's purposes for church are not being accomplished in your family, then your comfort will bring little consolation.

3. What should I do if the church we attend isn't helping our children grow?

Mary and Joseph did not dump their responsibility on the church.

It's ultimately your responsibility, not the church's, to teach your children God's Word and raise them God's way. If you're already attending a good Bible church where your family has strong community, but the teaching and support that your children are receiving is a little weak, try to think of other ways to strengthen the support before you entertain a move. Talk to the people in charge and see if there is some way that you and other volunteers can help. In many churches, the children's programs suffer only because they don't have enough staff and volunteers to do the job well.

See if the church has any mid-week clubs that teach the Bible for your children. Perhaps you could do some research and find out if better curricula exist, then helpfully share your findings with the church leaders. Be very careful that you keep a helpful, submissive attitude, and make sure that you go willing to work and help, if needed. The quickest route to being ignored is to be critical.

4. What if my spouse and I were raised in two different churches, or just disagree about which church to attend?

Mary and Joseph came to agreement and acted as one parent.

This one is simple to resolve. Read this chapter together and agree to work together to solve the problem. If you see from God's Word the purpose for church and set your "selection criteria" accordingly, this problem will usually become a moot point. It's not about going to the church of your childhood or the church where your spouse feels more comfortable; it has to be about community support and you and your children being taught the Word of God effectively. Both of you need to agree to move your personal preferences to the bottom of the "selection criteria" list.

5. What should I do if my child doesn't want to go to church?

Mary and Joseph obeyed God, not their children.

This is like asking, "What if my child doesn't want to eat or brush his teeth or be nice to his sister?" Going to church is part of God's plan, and obeying him is not an option if we want his best. So long as your children are children, then not attending church should never be considered an option.

Having said that, I don't think we should ever just tell them that they're coming whether they like it or not, just because we said so. Spend time with your child and explain again the importance and practical purpose for church. Ask them why they don't want to go, then listen carefully with an ear to God. It's actually quite normal for children to feel this way at some point, and their objections usually stem from something simple, like they have to get up too early on Sunday morning, they're bored in the class they go to, or they're having peer problems. Once you discover the root of the problem, see if you can do something about it. Go to a later service, see if your child can move to a more challenging class, help him build stronger relationships by letting him invite a few of the children over for fun outside of church.

Our children need to eat their vegetables, but we try our best to make it easy by picking ones that they prefer and by using recipes that will make the food taste good. In the same way, along with teaching its importance, try and make their church experience an enjoyable one. Make a habit of going to their favorite restaurant after church, or stop and get a slushy on the way home. Work at making Sunday morning preparations as enjoyable and stress free as possible. Saturday evening preparation really helps with this. If your children enjoy a certain breakfast that they don't get often, serve it Sunday morning.

The Greek word for *synagogue* comes from a common word meaning to gather. We need to follow Joseph's family's example, and synagogue together every week.

Practical Parenting **TIPS** *For Today*

Church attendance is one area where your actions will speak much louder than your words. If your family gets up and goes to church every Sunday, it will be a normal part of family life for your child. If you go sporadically, your child will question the importance of regular church attendance. If church becomes an outlet for a relationship with God, then that relationship will spill over into relationships with other Christians, and church attendance will become something to look forward to, not to dread.

CHAPTER 49

Jesus and Children:

Bringing Your Child to Jesus

*J*esus knew from experience what it's like to be a kid, to grow up God's way, and to have God as his Third Parent. Jesus knew God's Word and God's purposes and plans for how children were to be raised, and he personally and intimately knew how much God loves children and wants to be part of their lives.

Every time Jesus came in contact with children, he taught how important they are to God and how important it is to bring them to Him, to protect them from sin and going the world's way, and to teach and train them.

He once issued a dire and impassioned warning to anyone who would lead children away from God:

> *"But if anyone causes one of these little ones who believe in me to sin, it would be better for him to have a large millstone hung around his neck and to be drowned in the depths of the sea."* (Matthew 18:6)

Jesus didn't merely say that such an offender would be better off being thrown in the sea, an ancient form of capital punishment; he painted a much more definitive picture. The offender was to have a millstone tied around his neck—not a small household version, but a large millstone, the kind that took a beast of burden to move. The millstone wasn't to be tied to a leg, but to the neck; and the offender was to be cast not merely into the sea, but into the deepest part of the sea. Jesus knew how to make a point, and the language he used clearly demonstrated how much he wanted us to pay attention to his words.

After a brief recess, Jesus returned to his topic of children:

> *"See that you do not look down on one of these little ones. For I tell you that their angels in heaven always see the face of my Father in heaven. What do you think? If a man owns a hundred sheep, and one of them wanders away, will he not leave the ninety-nine on the hills and go to look for the one that wandered off? And if he finds it, I tell you the truth, he is happier about that one sheep than about the ninety-nine that did not wander off. In the same way your Father in heaven is not willing that any of these little ones should be lost."*
> (Matthew 18:10–14)

Jesus taught that God has assigned angels to children to help them come to him; but when we "look down on them," thinking them unimportant because they're "just children" and therefore not worth discipling, then they wander away. Now the shepherd must leave the flock and go searching for that person and try to bring them back as an adult. How much easier would it be if we didn't "look down on them," but saw raising them God's way as essential and helped the little ones not to wander off in the first place!

Millions of adults have been won to Christ, and God, through the power of the Holy Spirit, will continue to look for every lost sheep. Remember Proverbs 22:6, though. When people aren't raised to learn the truth and being trained to live their lives God's way, then they learn the world's way. God wired us so that what we learn as children becomes our default response, so that people who come to Christ as adults need to relearn how to think, respond, feel, and act (Romans 12:2).

Retraining is a long process, far more difficult than training children right the first time. Jesus knew that raising children God's way has always been, and still is, God's plan. Having a person wander away, only to be rescued later in life, is clearly Plan B.

As parents, we do our best and sometimes our children will still make the wrong choice. And even if we didn't know better at the time, it's never too late to start. We need to take Jesus' teaching seriously and, with his help, actively and purposefully teach and train our children to steer clear of sin.

Most people, when asked to name a time that Jesus got upset, would mention when he overturned the tables of the money changers in the temple. But if you read Mark 10:13–16, you'll find another one—the story about children coming to Jesus.

Jesus and his disciples were spreading the word about God's kingdom. The disciples were more than likely doing crowd control, keeping things orderly and making sure Jesus didn't get mobbed. Some people started bringing children to Jesus, and the disciples must have seen this as a waste of Jesus' time. After all, Jesus is important and his time should be spent ministering to adults, right?

Wrong!

When Jesus saw them rebuking those who were trying to bring children to him, he became indignant. He didn't just say, "Ah, aren't they cute. Let them come here for a minute so I can do a photo-op." He felt indignant—angry, incensed, and annoyed. The amplified translation of the Bible uses the word *pained* for how Jesus reacted. I like how he explained his reaction:

> *He said to them, "Let the little children come to me, and do not hinder them, for the kingdom of God belongs to such as these."* (Mark 10:14)

Jesus knew that God intended—and still does—for every person to get to know God and grow up with God from childhood. In essence, he said to his disciples, "Hey, what are you doing? We're out here preaching the kingdom of God— and the ideal candidates, those who can come when God intended them to come, show up—and you try to chase them off?" Then he said, *"I tell you the truth, anyone who will not receive the kingdom of God like a little child will never enter it."*

Often people use this verse to encourage adults to have simple, childlike faith. That's a good secondary application, but in context, Jesus is still talking about the children. Jesus was affirming that God created us to come to him as children by saying that, in order for adults to come to him, he has to reprogram us to receive him as we would have as a child.

God wants adults, everywhere, to come to him through Christ; but he desires each of us to know him from childhood. The kingdom of God belongs to our children, and we need to follow the example of those in this story who brought their children to Jesus.

Each of us should pray for the salvation of our children and actively move them in that direction, looking forward to the day when they climb on Jesus' lap in their hearts and receive him as their Lord and Savior. Jesus died for everyone, but each of us needs to make a personal decision to accept the gift—and that includes our children (Romans 10:9–10).

Here are some practical tips for preparing your child for that day:

1. *Read them the Story.* From the time your children are old enough to listen, read them Bible stories every day. Focus on Jesus and his story. At Christmas and Easter, use the anticipation that builds up during the preceding weeks to read daily and teach your children about the details and meaning of these holy holidays.

2. *Explain the message.* Your children need to become familiar with the story, but they also need to know why Jesus died, what that has to do with them, and what they can do about it. Keep it simple, but be ready to answer their questions.

3. *Wait for God's moment when your child is ready.* Pray for them, read the story, teach the message, and answer their questions, all with an ear toward God. The time will come when you will know in your heart what to do; some children ask if they can accept Jesus; some parents just feel the time is right and ask their child; sometimes it happens at church—there is no exact recipe for salvation. Your child coming to Christ is something very personal between her and God. God will use you in the process and he wants you to be active in doing your part, but let God remain in control.

4. *Continue to reinforce and explain your child's salvation.* Being born into God's kingdom is just the beginning of a

long, wonderful, growing relationship with our heavenly Father. Jesus died to restore us to the Father so that we could live and grow in his will and care for us. Jesus needed to die for our sins in order to clear away the obstacle that stood in the way of the goal.

5. *Make it memorable.* Children can understand enough to respond to Jesus' sacrifice for them. Help make a memory of the event by having a gathering of family, friends, and other Christians or a special meal. The Bible says that the angels in heaven celebrate when someone comes to Christ; why not share in the celebration on earth? It's good to record the day and events around the salvation of your young children so that you can tell them the story when they grow older.

Sin separates every one of us from God. The penalty for sin is death. Jesus had no sin of his own; that's why he could die in our place. Even though Jesus died for the sins of the whole world, each of us must decide for ourselves if we will accept this gift. To accept it, we simply go to God in prayer and ask him to forgive all of our sins and make us his child because of what Jesus did for us. Then ask him to help us learn about him, get to know him, and live the way he wants us to (see Romans 10:9–10 and Acts 2:38).

God looks at the heart, not the specific words. When your child opens his heart to Jesus, he'll be right there, welcoming him with open arms.

Jesus died for us all, and what happens when we get transferred from the kingdom of darkness into the kingdom of Christ is very, very real—no matter what age we are when we make the trip.

"Let the little children come to me, and do not hinder them, for the kingdom of God belongs to such as these." (Matthew 19:14)

Practical Parenting
TIPS  *For Today*

Here are some verses that will help you answer your child's questions:

The Fall:
Genesis 3:1–15
Because of Adam's sin, all are sinners:
Romans 3:23; 5:18–21
The penalty of sin is death: Genesis 2:17;
Romans 6:23
Jesus talks about being born again: John 3:3
For God so loved the world: John 3:16
We can become God's children: John 1:12–13
Salvation is a free gift: Romans 6:23
How to be saved: Romans 10:9–10
The gift of the Holy Spirit: Acts 2:38; Romans 5:5
The importance of obedience: Matthew 28:19–20;
John 14:23
God is love: 1 John 4:8

When your child is ready to receive Christ as Savior, explain that when we want to apologize to someone or make up with them, we need to talk to them. In the same way, when we are ready to ask God to forgive our sins and make us his child because of what Jesus did, we need to talk to God in prayer. Help them pray a simple prayer that they can understand that incorporates this idea and the truths they've learned about salvation. Celebrate with your child when he or she makes this step, and don't forget to explain that this is only the first step in the wonderful journey of getting to know God.

CHAPTER 50

Peter and Paul Pass the Torch:

The Tale of Two Mission Fields

I started off in the introduction saying that the Bible bursts with instructions and examples—good and bad—for us to learn from. Well, if you've read the whole book, you know that's true. In fact, the more I dove into Scripture, the more practical teaching for parents I found tucked away in God's Word.

As we've noted throughout this book, God chose Abraham and trained him how to raise children who would love and follow God. God told Abraham to do this, and to train his children after him to do the same thing, so that they could enjoy the blessings of his promise to bless all nations through Abraham.

Abraham will surely become a great and powerful nation, and all nations on earth will be blessed through him. For I have chosen him, so that he will direct his children and his household after him to keep the way of the LORD *by doing what is right and just, so that the* LORD *will bring about for Abraham what he has promised him.* (Genesis 18:18–19)

God continued to emphasize the importance of raising godly children to Abraham's descendants, the Israelites, generation after generation. When they raised their children God's way, they flourished and grew; when they didn't, things went downhill.

God had the writers of the Bible record parenting teachings and parenting examples, good and bad, for the Israelites to learn from. God used all of these real-life lessons to help Mary and Joseph to raise God's only Son, his way.

God's instruction to Abraham and his descendants to raise their children God's way has now passed to spiritual Israel— Christians (see Galatians 6:16). If sin had not entered the picture, all of us would have only one harvest field: our children. Now that Jesus has died for everyone, the harvest field has grown to include the lost of the nations, but the original mandate to reach and teach our own children remains our responsibility. Also, God's promise to bless all nations is still in process, and raising our children God's way still has a large role to play in fulfilling that promise.

Raising children God's way involves a lot more than just adding a side order of religion to their lives—taking them to church, saying prayers before bed and mealtime, and reading them some Bible Stories. By itself, that won't cut it.

Paul wrote to the New Testament church: *"Fathers, do not exasperate your children; instead, bring them up in the training and instruction of the Lord"* (Ephesians 6:4).

We are to bring up our children in the training and instruction of the Lord. Christianity isn't just something we believe; it's about who we are, how we think, and how we behave. In order to bring up children God's way, we need to teach them what God's Instruction Manual for Life (the Bible) says about everything and train them to think, talk, and live according to God's Word. Quite possibly, Paul had in mind what Solomon wrote in Proverbs: *"Train a child in the way he should go, and when he is old he will not turn from it"* (Proverbs 22:6).

It sounds straightforward enough: bring a child up God's way, and when he's old enough to make choices on his own, he'll continue doing things that way. It makes sense on a very practical level.

If you've helped your child to understand obedience and ensured that she obeys legitimate authorities, then she knows it works and why; it's become her built-in response. If you've taught him to pray and rely on God and helped him to see the results, then he will default to prayer when he needs help and direction. They will continue to function in relationships in the way they've been taught, continue to be honest, continue to believe that the Bible is the source of truth, etc. What you've taught them and established in their lives is truth and it works. It would take more thought and effort to change those established beliefs and responses than to continue in them.

The Book of Proverbs is not a book of promises, but a book of life principles that, when applied properly, more often than not yield a bountiful and blessed harvest. So although believing in Jesus and taking your child to church is great, it doesn't automatically mean that God has promised to keep them in the faith. It does mean that if we train our children to walk out their Christian faith, we'll firmly establish them in the truth and they will tend to continue to live the same way.

All of the Old Testament teachings and examples that guided Mary and Joseph are still applicable today; we have the opportunity to bring our children to Jesus and, as Mary and Joseph did, raise them in God's special presence, with their heavenly Father helping us and them every step of the way.

In the New Testament, we see God pouring out his blessing and Spirit not only on adults, but on their children as well. Peter preached to the crowds on the day of Pentecost and explained:

> "No, this is what was spoken by the prophet Joel: 'In the last days, God says, I will pour out my Spirit on all people. **Your sons and daughters** will prophesy, your young men will see visions, your old men will dream dreams.'" (Acts 2:16–17, emphasis added)

A few verses later, he again spoke to the crowd about their children:

> Peter replied, "Repent and be baptized, every one of you, in the name of Jesus Christ for the forgiveness of your sins. And you will receive the gift of the Holy Spirit. The promise is for you and your children and for all who are far off—for all whom the Lord our God will call." (Acts 2:38–39, emphasis added)

Later, when God showed Peter that the gospel was for the Gentiles as well, the Holy Spirit was poured out on Cornelius and his household.

*"He told us how he had seen an angel appear in his house and say, 'Send to Joppa for Simon who is called Peter. He will bring you a message through which you and **all your household will be saved.**' "*

(Acts 11:13–14, emphasis added)

Further, when an earthquake set Paul and Silas free from prison, this is what happened:

*He then brought them out and asked, "Sirs, what must I do to be saved?" They replied, "Believe in the Lord Jesus, and you will be saved—**you and your household.**" Then they spoke the word of the Lord to him and to all the others in his house. At that hour of the night the jailer took them and washed their wounds; then immediately **he and all his family were baptized**. The jailer brought them into his house and set a meal before them; he was filled with joy because he had come to believe in God—**he and his whole family**.*

(Acts 16:30–34, emphasis added)

Again and again God shows us that outreach often happens with the whole household. God wants to reach the lost—both adults and children. Two mission fields, two very different programs for discipleship: the church trains the converts and the parents train their children.

God chose Abraham and Sarah and Mary and Joseph to raise children his way for a very important reason: to bring Jesus into the world and to establish an effective discipleship program for children.

Although in our society we've come to believe that the discipleship of our children is the church's job, it never has been and it still isn't. It has to fall to the parents, because children must be trained daily, in the midst of life.

If you realize that it's your responsibility, then ask for God's help (he never intended that you do it alone), start from where you are, and move forward one step at a time. Just get started; it's never too late!

And now, I join Paul in my parting challenge to you as parents and as members of the body of Christ:

> *It was he who gave some to be apostles, some to be prophets, some to be evangelists, and some to be pastors and teachers, **to prepare God's people for works of service**, so that the body of Christ may be built up until we all reach unity in the faith and in the knowledge of the Son of God and become mature, attaining to the whole measure of the fullness of Christ. Then we will no longer be infants, tossed back and forth by the waves, and blown here and there by every wind of teaching and by the cunning and craftiness of men in their deceitful scheming. Instead, speaking the truth in love, we will in all things grow up into him who is the Head, that is, Christ. From him the whole body, **joined and held together by every supporting ligament, grows and builds itself up in love, as each part does its work.***

(Ephesians 4:11–16, emphasis added)

Church leaders are to prepare the people who make up the church to do works of service that strengthen and build the church. The main "work of service" for building up the church for every Christian parent is the Christian discipleship of his or her children.

If you're already raising your children God's way, or if you're just getting started, I would like to challenge you to do your part to grow and strengthen the body of Christ. Share with other parents what you've learned and help them to get started. Perhaps you can even help in your church to equip other parents for the awesome task of raising God's children God's way.

As we work together and effectively reach and train both new converts and our own children, perhaps we'll see God's promise to Abraham completely realized as each generation of Christians on this earth becomes stronger.

> *"And this gospel of the kingdom will be preached in the whole world as a testimony to all nations, and then the end will come."* (Matthew 24:14)

Practical Parenting TIPS For Today

Just as Peter and Paul taught, your mission field is twofold: lost people in the world; and your own children. Know that Jesus takes very seriously your work to raise your children to become godly, Christian adults. Your home-grown mission field is as precious to him as the mission field on a faraway continent. Use the stories, the life lessons that God so graciously gave you in his Word, to parent intentionally, purposefully, and with the end in mind of seeing your children and many more with you in heaven.